W9-ARO-596

Wagner the Mystic

by

John J. Pohanka

For Maren, My colleague, friend and fellow Wagnerian

John
May 20, 2010

"Mysticism is the scholastic of the heart,

the dialectic of the feelings."

— Goethe

Copyright©2010 by John J. Pohanka

All rights reserved.

Published by:

The Wagner Society of Washington, DC
P.O. Box 58213
Washington, DC 20037

The Wagner Society of Washington, DC
www.wagner-dc.org

ISBN-10   0615366481
ISBN-13   9780615366487

Acknowledgements

My parents, Frank and Charlotte Pohanka, worked hard during the depression to provide me with the benefit of a solid private school education and then the experience of an exciting liberal arts program at Princeton University. There, philosophy professor Walter T. Stace, music professor Roy Dickinson Welsh and classics professor J. Whitney Oates introduced me to subjects which were entirely new to me, kindling in me a lifelong fascination with these fields.

The Wagner Society of New York and later the Wagner Society of Washington, D.C. introduced me to fellow Wagnerians and enabled a continuing study of Wagner and his great art.

J.K. Holman, Chairman of WSWDC, encouraged me to share with other members thoughts that I had regarding Wagner's mysticism. As a result, I delivered my first lecture on the subject to the Society at one of their monthly meetings.

Bryan Magee's wonderful books, *Aspects of Wagner, Schopenhauer,* and *The Tristan Chord*, had provided me with some of the most valuable information and background for my talk, and I sent to him in Oxford, England, a compact disc recording of it in hopes that he might listen to it and provide me with some reaction. Mr. Magee graciously replied with valuable criticism of my work and unexpected praise writing, "It is a major contribution to the study of Wagner." This encouraged me to continue and to expand my research on the subject.

Father Owen Lee in turn critiqued my talk, and his complimentary remarks gave me further encouragement to continue the development of my thesis that Wagner was a kind of mystic and was able to convey his mystical experience to others through his music.

Several versions of the resulting manuscript were read and critiqued by Jerome Sehulster, professor of psychology at the University of Connecticut, J.K. Holman, Speight Jenkins of the Seattle Opera, and Beth and Saul Lilienstein.

Beth Lilienstein's artistic insights were invaluable in developing the captions for the picture section.

Ken Howard, Winnie Klotz and Ul de Rico graciously allowed me to reproduce their photos and art work.

My assistant, Debra Matthews, spent countless hours deciphering my handwriting and putting everything in shape to go to the publisher.

The standards of scholarship and dedication examplified by my son, Brian Caldwell Pohanka, in his work as a historian were always on my mind, and it was the letter he wrote to me just before his death in 2005 encouraging me to finish my work and have it published that spurred me on to complete the project.

Table of Contents

Acknowledgements III

Table of Contents V

Preface VII

Chapter 1

Two Puzzles 1

Chapter 2

The Mystic State 7

Chapter 3

The Well Read Wagner 11

Chapter 4

Threads In The Wagner Fabric 15

Chapter 5

Schopenauer 33

Chapter 6

Tristan 41

Chapter 7

Eastern Influences 47

Photo Gallery

Staging Wagner's Mysticism 57

Chapter 8

The Wagner Moment: A Mystical Experience 73

Chapter 9

Wagner's Intentions 77

Table of Contents
(continued)

Chapter 10

   The Second Puzzle 89

Epilogue

   Wagner's Grail, His Great Art ......….................................….......... 93

Index 95

Bibliography 99

Notes 107

PREFACE

"The music simply swept over me like a tidal wave...It was self-discovery. I felt that I had touched something that, however impossible it may sound in words, was part of me. Something deep within this eleven-year-old music lover responded. It left me at a whole new level of awareness, astonished at the response that music could awaken in me. For years and years thereafter, Wagner's music was everything to me."
— Father Owen Lee, *(Wagner Moments)*

Like Father Owen Lee, my introduction to Wagner came through *Tannhäuser*. In February of 1946, at age seventeen, I traveled from Princeton to New York City to hear jazz played at Nick's in Greenwich Village. Walking down Broadway, I passed the old Metropolitan Opera House and noticed that they were performing *Tannhäuser*. Never having seen an opera, I thought that I would try it. Although I had no idea of what was going on, not realizing that a synopsis was in the program — and of course there were no surtitles — I was totally carried away by what I saw and heard. Although I had enjoyed going to the theatre, no theatrical performance combined so many elements in such a powerful way, and it transported my psyche to a place unknown to me before. I felt that I had either lost or discovered my identity, maybe both, while at the same time I was set free and became part of some other world or place. It was a wonderful feeling, and I was anxious to have more or it.

The magic of that experience lives with me to this day and, indeed, has been repeated countless times while listening to Wagner's music. Finding, over the years, that many other people have had similar experiences set me on a quest to try to determine why this happens, did Wagner intend it to happen, and, if so, why?

In discovering a book, *Mysticism and Philosophy* by my old Princeton philosophy professor, Walter T. Stace, forty years after my first

Tannhäuser, I found clues which I felt could help me answer these questions. My excitement grew as I delved further into the extensive Wagner literature finding information which seemed to confirm my thoughts that what many of us feel when listening to Wagner's music is a kind of mystical experience which Wagner much wanted us to have.

This is not a book for everyone. After all, some people don't care for Wagner's music, and some can take it or leave it. But Wagnerians will understand and hopefully gain additional insight into their own feelings. As for those readers who have had little contact with Wagner, I hope that this book will encourage them to get involved and come to experience Wagner the mystic.

WAGNER THE MYSTIC

CHAPTER ONE

TWO PUZZLES

In February, 1860, the French poet, Charles Beaudelaire, after attending a concert of music from *Tannhäuser*, wrote to Richard Wagner, the composer, as follows:

> "What I felt is indescribable, and if you will deign not to laugh, I will try to translate it for you...You immediately felt carried away, under a spell...I often experienced quite a strange feeling, the pride and enjoyment of understanding, of being engulfed, overcome, a really voluptuous sensual pleasure, like riding into the air or being rocked on the sea...In general those deep harmonies reminded me of those stimulants which accelerate the pulse of the imagination...There is everywhere something elevated and everlasting, something reaching out beyond, something excessive, something superlative...this would be if you like, the final paroxysm of the soul...you have brought me back into touch with myself and with greatness."[1]

Charles Beaudelaire may have been one of the first persons to try to describe the indescribable, the impact of Wagner's music on people, but he was far from the last. For some reason Wagner's music has impacted its audiences in a strange mystical type of way for over one hundred and fifty years. Not every listener, of course, is affected, but an astonishing number of them are. These are not the typical type of aesthetic experiences that one might get in looking at a great painting. Those do not have the intensity or the length of intensity that can occur in listening to Wagner's music.

The Wagnerian scholar, J.K. Holman, in his book, *Wagner Moments,* records over one hundred such experiences originating from a wide variety of people including singers, authors, composers, musicians and ordinary lay people. Holman defines a Wagner moment as "that 'aha' moment when one first connected with Wagner, possibly in a way that has consequences." As chairman of the Wagner Society of Washington, D.C., Holman has presented a host of Wagnerian scholars lecturing to the Society's membership over the past ten years. It is a Society tradition to invite the lecturer, anyone accompanying him and also new members, to an informal dinner at a nearby Chinese restaurant after the lecture. Routinely these people are asked, "Tell us about your Wagner moment." I have attended many of these events and am continually amazed and am continually amazed by the fascinating stories told by these people, each one relating how Wagner's music touched them in a significant way. It is unfortunate that none of the fascinating stories told by these people were recorded. Now that, due to Holman's book, the phrase "Wagner Moment" is becoming part of the vernacular, the recording of additional Wagner moments undoubtedly will be forthcoming.

Many of the experiences like Beaudedaire's seem to have metaphysical or mystical connotations. To reference just a few in Holman's book, Chris Hunter, "My whole being had been lifted to another place";[2] Claude DeBussy, "You are no longer yourself";[3] and Jeffrey Swann, "I was discovering something new, on the outside, but I was recognizing something that had been there all along, on the inside, and it was becoming manifest."[4]

To better understand all this, it is important to have a clear understanding of metaphysics and mysticism. Webster defines metaphysics as follows: "Metaphysics – made up of ontology: What is reality? And epistemology: How do we access it?

The answer to these questions might seem relatively simple. Reality is this chair, this room, the trees outside, etc. We access this reality through our senses. We touch it, see it, hear it, smell it, and so forth. For philosophers, however, things are not that simple. Many philosophers feel there is another world – a world not accessible to our senses.

As for Mysticism, Webster defines it as: "A belief in, or reliance on, the possibility of spiritual apprehension, of knowledge inaccessible to the intellect." The phrase "inaccessible to the intellect", is very important to mystics in the development of their own metaphysical thinking.

Bryan Magee in his book, *Aspects of Wagner*, writes about Wagner's music as follows:

"Some people are made to feel by it...that they are in touch with the depths of their own personality for the first time. The feeling is of wholeness yet unboundedness – hence, I suppose, its frequent comparison with mystical or religious experience."

When I first read this passage over forty years ago, I felt that Magee had done a very good job of putting into words what I experienced when I first came into contact with Wagner's music at the age of seventeen, an experience that has been repeated many times since. This business of "wholeness yet unboundedness" is a paradox. In getting in touch with the depths of our personality we have a feeling of wholeness, yet we have a feeling of being set free from our own individuality, the unboundedness, becoming one with something else out there. In Beaudelaire's words it is a "reaching out beyond".

It is very difficult to put this kind of experience into words. It is, in effect, ineffable. Beaudelaire says "What I felt is indescribable". Yet it is there. It is objective, not subjective; it isn't a dream. This is happening to us when we experience it, and it is certainly real.

Magee goes on to say that some people are revolted by the Wagner experience. "To them Wagner's music is the voice of the prohibited; it speaks out to their forbidden selves. And so they denounce it in moral terms – 'dangerous', 'disgusting', 'vulgar', 'excessive', 'self-indulgent', 'sick'."[6]

Michael Tanner reaches a conclusion similar to Magee's: "It is satisfying to Wagnerians to feel that they can cope with uniquely explicit revelations of their unconscious. And it is satisfying to anti-Wagnerians to feel that they are rejecting the glorification of barbaric forces."[7]

The eminent Wagner scholar, Father Owen Lee agrees:

"The fact that Wagner's dreams plunge us through myth and music deep into ourselves, and what we discover there – often primitive, frightening, vindictive, and erotic – are the feelings that we who have constructive roles in society have suppressed. We may have relegated those desires beneath the level of consciousness, but none of us has completely tamed them. Many of those who detest Wagner do so because they realize that his music reaches that subconscious level as no other music does."[8]

People react very strongly to Wagner's music, and the anti-Wagnerians can be as eloquent as those who have experienced Wagner Moments. Friedrich Nietzsche, one of Wagner's most ardent disciples in the early stages of their friendship, later turned on his friend. In *Nietzsche Contra Wagner* he wrote:

"Apparently you think that all music must leap out of the wall and shake the listener to his very intestines. Only then do you think composed music is effective. Whereas on whom are such effects achieved, on those a mature artist would never impress, on the mass, on the immature, on the blasé, on the sick, on the idiots, on the Wagnerians."[9]

In reviewing *Tristan*, the critic Eduard Hanslick wrote "The prelude to *Tristan und Isolde* reminds me of the old Italian painting of a martyr whose intestines are slowly unwound from the body on a reel."(10)

Yet the popularity of Wagner continues to grow. Wagner societies abound throughout the world – groups of people who meet on a regular basis to dissect, discuss and debate every aspect of Wagner's life and works. One rarely finds Verdi societies, or Mozart societies, or Puccini societies despite the popularity of their operas. But there are over one hundred forty registered Wagner Societies worldwide from Beijing to Zagreb.

Since it's founding by Wagner in 1876, the Feistspielhaus in Bayreuth, Germany, has produced only Wagner operas, and people must wait for years to obtain tickets, this despite some over-zealous producers who mutilate Wagner's operas by distorting the stories and placing them in locations totally foreign to Wagner's conceptions.

Ring cycles seem to be growing like mushrooms, springing up all over the world despite the expense in staging them and the extreme difficulty in finding singers who can perform them. At a time when time is so precious to everyone, people travel great distances to spend eighteen hours over a six day period to immerse themselves in Wagner's tale of Gods, giants, dwarfs and humanity. The Seattle *Ring* in 2005 was attended by people from thirty-five states and forty-two countries.

And so the number of people experiencing the mysticism of Wagner's music continues to expand.

Ever since reading Magee I have been struggling to solve what for me is the puzzle of the Wagner moment? Why do these experiences happen? Did Wagner intend them to happen? And if so, why? This book is a continuation of that struggle.

For some years prior to reading Magee I had been working on solving a different Wagnerian puzzle. While taking Professor Roy Dickinson Welsh's course dealing with Wagner's life and works at Princeton University in 1947 I happened upon a letter from Richard Wagner to Friedrich Nietzsche written in February of 1870. Nietzsche had been sending Wagner copies of his lectures on Socrates. These lectures eventually became *The Birth of Tragedy out of the Spirit of Music*, Nietzsche's first book of any consequence. It was basically a hymn of praise to Wagner. Wagner liked what Nietzsche had sent him and wrote back to Nietzsche as follows:

> "Now you have the opportunity of proving the utility of philology by helping me bring about the grand renaissance in which Plato will embrace Homer. And Homer, imbued with Plato's spirit, will become, more than ever before, the supreme Homer."[11]

What is "the great renaissance", and why the combination of Homer and Plato? In all my research I have only seen this letter referred to twice. Ernest Newman mentions it briefly in his biography of Wagner, and Father Owen Lee in his *Athena Sings: Wagner and the Greeks*, refers to it one time. As years have gone by, I have come to think that there might be a relationship between the answers to the "Wagner moment puzzle" and to the "great renaissance puzzle", but more on that later.

CHAPTER TWO

THE MYSTIC STATE

In 1902 the philosopher William James wrote as follows:

"The overcoming of all unusual barriers between the individual and the Absolute is the great mystic achievment. In mystic states we become one with the Absolute and we become aware of our oneness. This is the everlasting and triumphant mystical tradition hardly altered by differences of clime or creed. In Hinduism, in Neo-Platonism, in Sufism, in Christian mysticism, in Whitmanism, we find the same recurring note, so that there is about mystical utterances an eternal unanimity which ought to make the critic stop and think."[12]

In 1960 the philosopher Walter T. Stace in his monumental study of mysticism, *Mysticism and Philosophy*, discovered that there are seven characteristics common to all mystical states regardless of the time, culture or place including the one that James had mentioned. Coincidentally, while an undergraduate at Princeton at the same time that Professor Roy Dickinson Welsh was fueling my interest in Wagner, Professor Stace introduced me to philosophy and in particular to the metaphysics and the dialogues of Plato. Forty years later I discovered *Mysticism and Philosophy* in a Madison Avenue bookstore.

The preeminent religious studies scholar, Huston Smith in his forward to the 1987 reprint of *Mysticism and Philosophy* wrote: "Incredible as it seems, Stace's book was completed not only in the heyday of analytic philosophy but in the bowels of the most prodigious American stronghold, the philosophy department of Princeton University...that a study of mysticism of this order emerged not from a cloister but from a hardheaded department of analytic philosophy, countering at every turn the prejudice against mysticism (and religion generally) that encrusted these departments in Stace's day, leaves one pondering which should be credited more, the independence and objectivity of its author in following the evidence where it led him or the power of the subject to stand its ground in the face of biases that work to bend it out of shape?"[13]

Smith considered the book a "classic" in that the substantial changes that transformed philosophy since its publication twenty-three years before "left Stace's substantive findings untouched."

Incredibly in his book Stace reached the conclusion "that mystical experience is in very truth what the mystics themselves claim, namely a direct experience of the One, the universal Self. God."[14] (Terminology varies with the culture.)

Stace's seven characteristics are as follows:

1. *The Unitary Conscious, the One the Void.*
   William James describes this as becoming one with the Absolute and being aware of the oneness. Stace describes it as the "the experience of the fading away or the breaking down of the boundary walls of the finite self so that his personal identity is lost and he finds himself merged or dissolved in an infinite or universal ocean of being... It is the nuclear and essential characteristic of all mystical experience."[15]

2. *Non spatial – non temporal.*
   The experience of the unitary consciousness, the One, the Void "must necessarily be spaceless and timeless, because space and time are the very conditions and exemplars of multiplicity."[16]

3. *Sense of objectivity or reality.*
   "The experience is immediately interpreted by the mystic of having objective reference and not being a mere

inner and subjective state of mind...his experience is not a mere dream – a something which is shut up entirely in his own consciousness."(17)

4. *Blessedness and peace.*

   It is a pleasant experience. The mystic has a feeling of blessedness, joy, peace, happiness bliss.

5. *Feeling of being sacred or divine.*

   Closely aligned with blessedness and peace, it has religious or spiritual connotations.

6. *Paradoxicality.*

   The paradox of the dissolution of individuality in which the 'I' both disappears and persists" is a "logical contradiction."(18)

7. *Alleged by mystics to be ineffable.*

   This is due to "a basic and inherent logical difficulty, and not due to mere emotional intensity."(19) Despite the fact that they feel it is ineffable, mystics of all ages struggle to find the words to describe their experience in order to share it with others.

Stace points out that not all of the seven characteristics might be reported in any one mystical experience. Different individual mystics will emphasize different aspects of their experiences depending on their temperament, circumstances, etc.

Each of Stace's seven characteristics of the mystic experience can be found in the life and works of Richard Wagner.

CHAPTER THREE

THE WELL-READ WAGNER

Wagner was the most intellectual, the most well-read, of all the great composers. His interests were widespread – philosophy, politics, history, drama, literature, myth, language, religion, poetry, music. Ernest Newman said that such a combination had never existed before; it has never happened since and, in all probability, it will never happen again. In 1841 when Wagner was twenty-eight years old and living in Paris, the composer Meyerbeer, in recommending Wagner for director of the Dresden Opera, attested to Wagner's wide knowledge of literature.

By 1847 Wagner had amassed a library of over 400 carefully selected volumes. The biographer, William Ashton Ellis and C.J. Glasenapp, describes Wagner's library as "quite exceptional in its content...An historian might have selected those books on ancient national customs, a philologist those on myth and saga, a sculptor or architect those on the plastic arts, and a poet that treasury of epics and dramas." A partial list of books in this library includes all the Greek dramatists in German translation: the collected works of Aeschylus, Sophocles, Euripides, and Aristophanes. Also, the collected works of Shakespeare, Molière, Hugo, Calderon, Goethe, Schiller, Lessing, and Kleist, plus the writings of Homer, Pindar, Xenophon, Herodotus, Thucydides, Demosthenes, Plutarch, Plato, and Aristotle, Chaucer, Gibbon, Byron, Le Sage, Rousseau, Cervantes, Hans Sachs, Tieck, and Heine.

Ellis and Glasenapp add that "In literature Wagner knew everything worth knowing, from the works of olden time down to the newest products of even so-called 'elegant' school; to the astonishment of his friends , who even here could never , or but rarely, introduce a novelty to him; whatever one broached, he knew about it already, and had taken up a standpoint towards it."[20]

Later in life while living in Wahnfried, his home in Bayreuth, Wagner had over 2500 volumes in his library, and these books did not just sit on the shelf. He was constantly reading and dissecting them, telling anyone who would listen to him about the things he had read and their importance.

Fortunately, his wife, Cosima, kept diaries in the last fourteen years of Wagner's life, from 1869 to 1883, describing their daily discussions involving a wide range of authors and subjects. A partial list involves Homer, Sophocles, Aeschylus, Xenophon, Sappho, Plato, Aristophanes, Euripides, Thucydides, Plutarch, Herodotus, Demosthenes, Ovid, Lucretius, The Edda, *The Volsunga Saga, The Nibelungen Lied, The Fritjof Saga, The Vilkina Saga*, Gottfried von Strassburg's *Tristan*, Hartmann von der Aue's *Poor Heinrich, Old Italian Fables, Indian Fairy Tales, The Upansihads*, Calderon, Cervantes, Lope de Vega, Dante, the whole of Shakespeare, nearly all of Goethe and Schiller, Voltaire, Balzac, Hugo, Beaumarchais, Byron, Carlyle, Gibbon, Scott, Lewes, Sterne, Darwin, The letters of Frederick the Great, Eckermann's *Conversations with Goethe*, Mone's *German Heroic Sagas*, Ranke's *History of France*, Burckhardt's *History of the Renaissance in Italy*, Grimm's *German Mythology*, Koppen's *History of Buddhism*, Muller's the *Dorians*, Nohl's *Gluck*, Nohl's *Beethoven*, Uhland's *History of Heroic Poetry*, Freytag's *Pictures from the German Past*, Devrient's *Mendelssohn*, Justi's *Winckelmann*, Lessing, Tieck, Hoffmann, Schopenhauer, Nietzsche, Keller, Raimund, Kleist, Hebbel, Heinse, Chamisso, Holderlin, Turgeniev, Gogol, Tolstoy, Eckhart and Taller.[21]

Wagner constantly was trying to articulate the wide variety of thoughts and ideas gestating in his head – much of it intuitively. As Alan David Aberback says in *The Ideas of Richard Wagner*, "Wagner had an insatiable need to make himself understood, first of all to himself, and then, if possible, to others."[22] He was obsessed with this and produced over fifteen volumes of prose works. Much of it is difficult reading and somewhat abstruse. Sentences often seem to go on forever as if

Wagner was trying to discover his own thoughts, which he probably was. Wagner was very much aware of, and frustrated by, his difficulty in getting his complex and ever-evolving thoughts down on paper. In his preface to *Music of the Future* written in 1860, Wagner describes his difficulties in writing:

> He cannot bring to it the required calm composure of the professional theoretician; rather, he is impelled by a passionate impatience which prevents him from giving the necessary time and attention to matters of style; he wants to put into every sentence the picture of the whole that is constantly in his mind; he doubts whether he has succeeded and the doubt drives him to make attempt again, so that eventually he works himself into a state of irritation and excitement completely unknown to the theoretician. Aware of all the error and failure, and upset still further by his awareness of it, he hurriedly finishes off his work, telling himself with a sigh that when all is said and done he can only expect to be understood by one who already shares his artistic standpoint.(23)

People lament that Wagner spent so much time writing rather than composing, but these exercises were a very important part of Wagner's intellectual and creative development. Without them he would never have been the creative artist that he was.

He became interested in serious reading at an early age – at age nine. He was fortunate that Germany had changed its education from one based on science to one based on classics. So at age nine he was studying Greek, Latin, Ancient History and Mythology. In his autobiography Wagner wrote that at age thirteen he translated the first twelve books of *The Odyssey* from Greek into German. There is some question as to the accuracy of that claim. The school records seem to indicate that he had translated the first three books and that he was the only student in the class to have done so. Before he was sixteen, he taught himself English so he could read Shakespeare in the original. This was no ordinary student. We know from Cosima that as years went by, that they had what they called their "indispensables". The list is interesting...Homer, Aeschylus, Sophocles, *The Symposium* of Plato, *Don Quichotte*, the whole of Shakespeare and Goethe's *Faust*.

I'll touch on some of the works and philosophies that Wagner came across, but only to the degree that they deal with the subject – Wagner the Mystic. In doing this, I think it's important to know what Fichte, the philosopher, said..."that each of us has the philosophy he has, because he is the person that he is."[24] The writers and the people who influenced Wagner, did so because Wagner was the kind of person that he was. Somebody else being exposed to the same things might have reacted quite differently. Many of the important ideas which Wagner came into contact with in his readings were concepts that he already had developed intuitively, and in many cases, he already had articulated them.

Over a period of time, Wagner developed his own metaphysics, thoughts as to what constitutes reality and how to access it, and very definitely a feeling for mysticism: the belief in the possibility of the spiritual knowledge inaccessible to the intellect. My thesis is that in the process, Wagner became a type of mystic himself, but unlike other mystics, Wagner was able to convey his vision to others through his art.

In tracing this development one finds that there are certain common threads, many of which were present in his early years and remained throughout the entire Wagner fabric. Each of them contain elements of Stace's seven characteristics of the mystic experience.

CHAPTER FOUR

THREADS IN THE WAGNER FABRIC

Wagner did not do anything on a small scale. He sought what was universal, eternal, and timeless. This is an important thread that runs through all of Wagner's works. This thread, along with other important threads, knit together to make up the Wagner fabric.

In 1834, at the age of twenty-one, he wrote, "the essence of dramatic art, is not consistent with a specific subject or a point of view, but in this: That the inner kernel of all human life, and action, the Idea, be grasped and brought to show."(25) W. Ashton Ellis in a footnote to his translation of Wagner's prose works notes that the Idea (with a capital I) is a reference to Plato's mystical world of Ideas.

In 1840, at age twenty-seven, Wagner wrote "what music expresses is eternal, infinite, and ideal. It speaks none of the passion, love, and longing of this or that individual, in this or that situation, but of passion, love, and longing in themselves."(26) Unknown to Wagner, two years earlier, another German, Arthur Schopenhauer, had written almost those exact same words.

So Wagner turned to mythology where the universal can be found, and archetypes can be found. He wrote in *Opera and Drama*, "the incomparable thing about a myth, is that it is true for all time, and its content inexhaustible throughout the ages. The poet's task was simply to interpret it"(27)

The first sentence of this quote is often found in books about Wagner, but the second sentence, which seldom is included, is important as well. In interpreting the myths Wagner put his own spin on the tales. Indeed, the same may be said of Homer, since classical experts today think that before the *Iliad* and *Odyssey* eventually were written down, they had undergone modifications by bards reciting the stories over the years. At the same time, the core of the story remains the same. Thus, from Cosima's diary..."Richard said what gives Homer's poetry – its stamp of eternity, is that every episode has a mythical quality. It is not an arbitrarily invented adventure."[28]

Wagner's interest in the universal, the eternal, the timeless led him to another important thread in the Wagner fabric – other-worldliness, a type of metaphysics. Wagner had read all the dialogues of Plato including *The Republic*, a metaphysical work presenting Plato's views on ontology and epistemology. It is here that Wagner discovered the world of Ideas.

In *The Republic,* the everyday world of the senses and of time and space is portrayed as being incomplete and unsatisfactory. But there is another world outside of time and space – the real world – the world of ideas. For example, a table in the world of senses is a table only in that it partakes of "the idea of table" in the world of ideas.

For the normal person, the real world of ideas is unreachable and unknowable. The closest he can get to it is through mathematics and through geometry in particular. Geometric forms like the square and right angle are definite and do not vary or change. However, there are no "perfect" squares or right angels in the world of senses, only in the real world of ideas.

The philosopher through knowledge (not feeling), and the use of the Socratic dialectic form of analysis leading to personal insight, can get in touch with the real world of ideas, although he will find it impossible to share his findings with others as it is incommunicable – ineffable. Even so, he should try his best to share this new knowledge.

To illustrate all this, Plato portrays man as being chained in a cave facing a wall. Behind man images are being carried, and a fire behind them throws shadows on the wall which man mistakenly thinks as being the real thing. This is the world of the senses, the world of space and time which values valor and honor over knowledge.

With the proper education including arithmetic, geometry, astronomy and music, the philosopher can break his chains and go to the mouth of the cave where he encounters the sun and the real world of Ideas (forms). When he returns to the cave to tell his fellow man what he has learned, he cannot see because of the darkness of the cave and is scorned by his fellow man as being ignorant. Plato is stressing the importance of the mind, the intellect. Feeling is not a factor.

Plato was greatly influenced by the thinking of Pythagoras and his followers. Pythagoras, who lived a century before Sophocles and Plato (582-507 BC), is best remembered for the Pythagorean theorem, $A^2 + B^2 = C^2$. The twentieth century mathematician and philosopher, A.N. Whitehead, described him as "the first thinker to appreciate the function of mathematical ideas in absolute thought."[29] He discovered that if you plucked a string to sound a note, then halved the length of the string, you would get the same note an octave higher. Two-thirds would result in an interval one-fifth higher, and so forth.

The curriculum suggested for the philosopher in *The Republic* (arithmetic, geometry, astronomy and music) is based on the quadrivivium developed by Pythagoras and his followers. Over the entrance to Plato's academy was a sign which read "Let no man enter who has not studied mathematics."

But Pythagoras was much more than a mathematician. He is known as the first scientist in Western civilization. He was the first person to call himself a philosopher – a lover of wisdom. He spent about twenty years in Egypt where he absorbed the mathematics and sciences of the Egyptians and also came into contact with pre-Buddhism thinking from India. Legend has it that he actually traveled to India. He and his followers believed in vegetarianism and reincarnation, doctrines which probably originated with his eastern contacts. Wagner eventually would embrace both these doctrines. Pythagoras also brought back from Egypt the Osiris religion which evolved into the Dionysic religion – the religion of Greece during the time of Socrates and Plato.

The Dionysic religion was based on gnosis – knowledge. "Gnothi Seauton" or "know thyself" was written on the sanctuary of Apollo at

Delphi. Gnosis, or knowledge, was self-knowledge. Every person had a lower self "eidalon" and a higher self "the Daemon". The goal through study of the "mysteries" was to bring the lower self into contact with the higher self causing a reunion. Through this enlightenment the initiate discovers there is a universal self (Daemon) which inhabits every human being, and to know that self is to know God. These pagan mysteries were a precursor of the Christian Gnostics, and there are vestiges of it today in the Masonic Lodge.

In *Religion and Art* written in1849 Wagner paid tribute to Pythagoras and the great impact he had on philosophical thinking: "No philosopher since him has pondered on the essence of the world without referring to his teaching."(30) Undoubtedly Wagner was aware of Plato's preoccupation in *The Republic* with gnosis, knowledge and reason, and mathematics. The problem that Wagner had with *The Republic*, is that Plato says the way to discover the eternal forms is through the intellect – through reasoning. Wagner, on the other hand, favored feeling as opposed to reasoning.

Also, in *The Republic*, Socrates expresses problems with Homer, Wagner's hero. The Homeric epics had become the basis of Greek education. Children learned how to read by studying Homer. Even cases in court were decided by doctrines portrayed in Homer. Socrates was concerned about the influence that Homer had on Greek life and the bad example set by his characters. He thought Homer's anthropomorphic treatment of the Gods to be particularly offensive:

> "We won't admit stories into our city – whether allegorical or not – about Hera being chained by her son, nor about Hephaestus being hurled from heaven by his father when he tried to help his mother, who was being beaten, nor about the battle of the gods in Homer. The young can't distinguish what's allegorical from what's not, and the opinions that they absorb at that age are hard to erase and apt to become unalterable."(31)

In reaction to Homer's rewarding people for unsavory acts, such as duplicity in the *Odyssey*, Socrates warns that "these stories are harmful to people who hear them, for everyone will be ready to excuse himself when he's bad."[32]

Moreover, Homer was from the heart, and Socrates and Plato were from the head. Homer talked about courage; Socrates talked about wisdom. As Socrates says to Glaucon in *The Republic*, "If you admit the pleasure-giving Muse, whether in lyric or epic poetry, pleasure and pain will be kings in your city instead of law or the thing that everyone has always believed to be best, namely, reason."[33]

In *The Symposium*, Wagner discovered a different kind of Plato. It is by far the most mystical of Plato's dialogues and develops the thought that platonic ideas can be discovered within the individual. It is significant that it was *The Symposium* which made it to the list of Wagner's "indispensables". Wagner said, "I read the best of Plato's Dialogues. It is only *The Symposium*, in particular, that I gained such an insight into the wonderful beauty of Greek life, that I felt myself palpably more at home in ancient Athens than any circumstances afforded by the modern world."[34]

To understand what Wagner meant by that, one has to know the story of *The Symposium*. Four or five Greeks like to go out, get drunk, and drink themselves under the table. They hire flute girls, who are prostitutes, and prepare to have a good time, and part of their definition of a good time involves the serious discussion of philosophy. Wagner, who certainly enjoyed a good time but would engage in serious philosophical discussions at the drop of a hat, felt a kinship with these Greeks.

This night they decide to discuss eros, or love. After some discussion, they are joined by Socrates who had been found "tranced" in the doorway of the next house. As the eminent Plato scholar A.E. Taylor points out, "Plato is plainly calling our attention to a marked feature in the character of Socrates. He is at heart a mystic and there is something 'other worldly' about him."[35]

Before he arrived, the discussion of eros dealt primarily with physical love, but when Socrates speaks he takes the high road. He says that love comes from appreciating the beautiful. You see a beautiful person, you love her, and what is really behind the eros is the quest for eternity. In making love and having children you are, in effect, having your progeny perpetuate your name – providing a kind of immortality.

But there is another kind of love, which is a spiritual one. Socrates points out that the results of physical love are not as fair or as enduring as the results of spiritual love.

Certainly Wagner had a need for physical love. He has been described as being over-sexed. But his need for a spiritual kind of love was just as great. In Matilda Wessendonk and Cosima, Wagner had two spiritual partners who could keep pace with his complicated thoughts and not only be good listeners but good contributors as well. In her diary for April 8, 1870, Cosima wrote "We read *The Symposium* until midnight; one of the deepest impressions of my whole life, as if I had seen the original beauty of which Diotima speaks. Tears of ravishment fill our eyes at the end of this wonderful poem."[36]

In Socrates story, Diotima, who is a Daemon (a Priestess in the Dionysic faiths) leads Socrates into a self-examination, discussion and discovery of beauty, and how it relates to eros. The philosopher must recognize the kinship in all beautiful bodies – physical or spiritual. Diotima leads Socrates up a ladder of the levels of beauty, first to see the beauty in the person, then to see the beauty in science, then the beauty in social institutions, and suddenly there's a revelation, of the eternal form of beauty itself, which is outside of time and space. "This Beauty is first of all eternal; it neither comes into being nor passes away; neither waxes nor wanes; next is not beautiful in part and ugly in part, nor beautiful at one time and ugly at another, nor beautiful in this relation and ugly in that, nor beautiful here and ugly there, as varying according to its beholders; nor again will this beauty appear to the imagination like the beauty of a face or hands or anything else corporeal, or like the beauty of a thought or science, or like beauty which has its seat in something other than itself, be it in a living thing or the earth or the sky or anything else whatsoever; he will see it as absolute, existing alone within itself, unique, eternal."(37) The apprehension of the eternal form of beauty is ineffable. Only in the intercourse with it, will the soul give birth to spiritual offspring, which is no shadow but substance.

This sudden revelation of the eternal form of beauty, is very important. A.E. Taylor, in his work *Plato the Man and His Works*, says: "It is this conviction that all knowledge about, is only preparatory to a direct *scientia visionis* – that Socrates reveals the fundamental agreement of his conception with that of the great mystics of all ages."(38) The metaphysical and mystical thought that the eternal forms could be found within the individual very much appealed to Wagner. It finds its way into all of Wagner's music dramas.

Albert Goldman in his book, *Wagner on Music and Drama* writes: Wagner's most original contribution to dramaturgy in the 19th century was the perfection of the demotivated drama, a drama that speaks to us in anagogical terms"...Let's stop right here. For most people, anagogy might be an unfamiliar word. Webster defines it as the "interpretation of a word, passage or text, that finds beyond the literal, allegorical and moral senses, a fourth and ultimate spiritual or mystical sense." (Back to the quote).

> "Wagner's most original contribution to dramaturgy in the 19th century was the perfection of the demotivated drama, a drama that speaks to us in anagogical terms and in which the story and characters are meant to serve as mediums between us and a larger, profounder, and truer world. Dramatists before Wagner – Byron, for example – had tried to do something similar, but Wagner provided his plays with a firmer philosophical basis by combining and amplifying the ideas

of early German romantics like Novalis, Gorres, Schelling, G.H. von Schubert, and the Schlegel brothers. In addition to regarding myths as the repositories of eternal truths and the folk as myth-makers, these German writers tended to share one key thought that is crucial for an understanding of the Wagnerian drama and influence in the last quarter of the nineteenth century. They assumed that the heart of the universe lay within each man's soul."(39)

Along with the threads of universality, and other worldliness or metaphysics, is the thread of redemption. Redemption plays an important role in Wagner's early operas, in fact, in all of his operas. The German word for redemption is "Erlœsung", which also means deliverance. Basically in these messages of redemption, or deliverance, Wagner's characters are seeking redemption or deliverance from this world into something much better – a mystical concept. "Eternal nothingness absorb me!"cries the Dutchman.

Bryan Magee points out in *The Tristan Chorde*, that the central characters in *The Flying Dutchman, Tannhäuser, Lohengrin*, and the *Ring*, "reject the world", and it is, in fact, "the aim and goal of everything in the main action."(40) Wagner here is saying that there is another world outside of time and space which is far better and truer than the world of illusion which we are forced to experience by the limitations of our own senses, and we should seek deliverance (erlœsung) from this false world and attain a type of union with the better and truer world – surely a metaphysical and mystical concept.

Allen David Aberback, in his, *The Ideas of Richard Wagner*, comments "in *The Flying Dutchman, Tannhäuser*, and *Lohengrin* Wagner demonstrated a deepening involvement with mystical and transcendental thoughts. By the late 1840's, Wagner's mystical bent was clearly a major element in his life. It carried him on a spiritual odyssey that continued through *Parsifal*."(41)

In 1845 Wagner was tired of working on *Tannhäuser* and went to Marienbad, a spa in Bohemia. He took some books with him for light reading. Included was a book on the Meistersingers, and Wolfram von Eschenbach's *Parsifal*. In the sixty days he was there, Wagner particularly was involved with exploring Grail legends

The Grail had a mystical quality about it, and at this point in time, Wagner's whole psyche was ready for this. It became an important part of the spiritual odyssey that Aberback talks about. Richard Cavendish says in his book, *The Legends of the Grail*, that "The Grail has an enthralling atmosphere of mystery. There are some tremendous secrets which stay tantalizingly just outside the mind's grasp in the shadows, beyond the edge of conscious awareness. The inner mystery of The Grail cannot be explained, because it is that which the heart of man cannot conceive nor the tongue relate."[42]

Although the grail experience may be an ineffable one, for centuries people have tried to describe it. The great mythologist, Joseph Campbell, describes grail legends as "timeless, telling not of miracles long past, but of miracles potential within ourselves, here, now, and forever." John Matthews, a renowned grail authority, adds that it is not the grail object itself that we are concerned with but "the actions of the Grail that we seek — the way it causes changes to happen — in the heart, in the mind, in the soul."[43]

Over the years, as Wagner sought to sort out his own complex ideas and feelings, it is easy to see why the grail and its power to transform was constantly on his mind.

In April of 1848 Wagner composed the Prelude to act one of *Lohengrin*. He had finished the entire opera before tackling the Prelude. Tanner writes:

> "He was the most intelligent and self-conscious, as
> well as the most intellectual of artists. Wagner could see
> that in the prelude he had written for *Lohengrin*, he had

written a different kind of music, one for which he had a dangerous gift – the gift of hypnosis."[44]

Certainly the Prelude is one of the most mystical things Wagner ever composed. Franz Liszt described it as "ethereal" with a character of "ideal mysticism".

Wagner felt the need to try to put in writing what the music was expressing. For a Wagner moment, try reading Wagner's description, or have someone read it aloud, while you listen to the Prelude:

"Out of the clear blue ether of the sky there seems to condense a wonderful yet at first hardly perceptible vision; and out of this there gradually emerges, ever more and more clearly, an angel-host bearing in its midst the sacred Grail. As it approaches earth, it pours out exquisite odours, like streams of gold, ravishing the senses of the beholder. The glory of the vision grows and grows until it seems as if the rapture must be shattered and dispersed by the very vehemence of its own expansion.

"The vision draws nearer, and the climax is reached when at last the Grail is revealed in all its glorious reality, radiating fiery beams and shaking the soul with emotion. The beholder sinks on his knees in adoring self-annihilation. The Grail pours out its light on him like a benediction, and consecrates him to its service; then the flames gradually die away, and the angel-host soars up again to the ethereal heights in tender joy, having made pure once more the hearts of men by the sacred blessing of the Grail."[45]

After attending a performance of *Lohengrin*, in Moscow in 1896, the Russian painter Wassily Kandinsky, decided to devote his life to art. He described his Wagner moment that day as follows:

"The violins, the deep tones of the basses, and especially the wind instruments at that time embodied

for me all the power of that pre-nocturnal hour. I saw all
my colors in my mind; they stood before my eyes. Wild,
almost crazy lines were sketched in front of me. I did
not dare use the expression that Wagner had painted
'my hour' musically."[46]

After composing the *Lohengrin* Prelude, Wagner felt the need to take
a deep breath before moving on. He went more than five years without
writing any more music – from April 1848 until November 1853, but
he was far from unoccupied during that period. They were five of
the busiest years of his life. Besides getting seriously involved in
the revolutionary uprisings in Dresden in 1849 and being forced to flee
Germany, Wagner was writing not music, but words, volumes of them.
He felt compelled to try to sort out the complex thoughts and feelings
whirling inside of him, and he read and wrote voraciously.

In 1848 and 1849 Wagner became seriously involved with the
writings of the philosopher, Ludwig Feuerbach. Undoubtedly, he was
acquainted with Feuerbachian concepts prior to then, probably in his
Paris years, since Feuerbach was the philosopher *du jour*. But in reading
Feurbach's *The Philosophy of the Future* in 1849, Wagner found thoughts
which were in tune with the revolutionary fervor Wagner was experiencing at that time and the transcendental and mystical thoughts
he was having. Wagner said, "I always regarded Feuerbach as the
radical release from the thraldom of accepted notions."[47] Those were
notions that dealt with religion, love, and politics. Actually, Feuerbach
said little about politics. It was the spin that Wagner and his friends
put on Feuerbach's writings.

Religion, though, was a very important part of what Feuerbach had
to say. "Beyond man and nature, there's nothing." In other words, Gods
don't exist, but they were invented by people to serve a good purpose.
God didn't create people, people created God. And people invent their
Gods in a form they would aspire to, eternal, omnipotent, and
omniscient. Interestingly enough, about 2000 years earlier, the Greek

philosopher Xenophanes, said something similar. In commenting on the immorality of Homer's gods he wrote with sarcasm:

> "Human beings think of the gods as having been born, wearing clothes, speaking and having bodies like our own. Ethiopians say the gods are black with snub noses. Thracians say they have blue eyes and red hair. If cows and horses had hands they would draw pictures of the gods looking like cows and horses."[48]

Some people feel that Wagner was anti-religious, but he was not anti-religious; he was anti-church. He shared Feuerbach's thought that one could learn a lot about people by studying their religions and did so all his life. Religion is an element in all of Wagner's operas from *The Flying Dutchman* through *Parsifal*.

The mystical or spiritual aspects of religion appealed to him – even aspects of the church service itself. It was the dogma of the church with which he disagreed. The church had done a poor job of conveying Jesus' message of love and compassion, and he, Wagner, eventually intended to do a far better job of that in his "stage-consecration festival drama" (Ein Bühnenweihfestspeil), *Parsifal*. In writing to King Ludwig regarding *Parsifal* in 1873, Wagner said, "I am inspired to write the work in order to preserve the world's profoundest secret, the truest Christian faith, to awaken that faith anew."[49]

He explained his use in *Parsifal* of religious symbols and aspects of church service in *Religion and Art* written in 1880 while he was composing the opera:

> "It is for art to salvage the essence of religion by construing the metaphysical symbols which religion wants us to believe to be literal truth in terms of their figurative value, so as to let us see their profound hidden truth through idealized representations. Whereas the priest is concerned only that the religious allegories should be regarded as factual truths, that is of no concern to the

artist, since he presents his work frankly and openly as his invention."(50)

The real message of *Parsifal* was that God is discovered not by going to church but through the mystical transcendence of love and compassion within the individual, and this process of enlightenment is available to anyone.

At the same time Wagner was reading Feuerbach he was reading the gospels and decided to sort out his thinking about Jesus and what Jesus' message was all about, by writing a proposed staged work, *Jesus of Nazareth*. In keeping with Feuerbach's thought that you can learn a lot about people by studying their religions, one can learn a lot about Wagner by studying what he had to say in *Jesus of Nazareth*.

In it he treats Jesus as a historical figure who was sent as a philosopher and teacher. Jesus talks about discovering God within the individual. "Your body is God's temple that in it he may delight...I bring man back into himself, in that he apprehendeth God in himself and not outside him...We are God himself, for God is knowledge of self."(51) This mystical concept is consistent with the idea expressed by Pythagoras, the Christian Gnostics, and Plato in *The Symposium*.

Wagner's Jesus shares Feuerbach's and Wagner's distrust of organized religion: "Every man who walketh in love is King and Priest in himself, for he is subject to no man but to God who dwelleth in him...no longer shall ye think to serve God by going to the temple, saying prayers and making sacrifices of things it pains man not to miss."(52)

Jesus expresses Wagner's mystical thoughts of deliverance (Erloesung), found in *The Flying Dutchman, Tannhäuser, and Lohengrin*:

"Life itself is the progressive divestment of his Me. Amends for the loss of Me comes only through the consciousness of his ascent into the generality, for only through his knowledge thereof, does he find himself again in the universal, and that enriched and multiplied; this consciousness of self or better, this becoming conscious of ourselves in the universe makes our life creative...first because by our abandonment of self we enrich the generality and in it our own selves."[53]

What Wagner is expressing here, the paradox of the dissolution of the individuality (the divestment of the Me) when this "Me" both disappears and exists in an enriched form as part of the generality, is one of the basic thoughts of mystics of all ages and cultures, as Stace describes it, "the nuclear and essential characteristic of all mystical experience."

While reading Feuerbach's brilliant book, *The Philosophy of the Future,* Wagner developed two more important threads: the idea of "becoming knowers through feeling" and the importance for man's unconscious to be raised to the level of consciousness.

These threads helped him resolve some of the problems he was having with his philosophical ponderings particularly in the area of metaphysics. He writes "I had always had an inclination to fathom the depths of philosophy, just as I had been led by the mystical influence of Beethoven's Ninth Symphony to search the deepest recesses of music. My first efforts at satisfying this longing failed." He had "racked his brains" trying to make something out of popular philosophers at that time such as Friedrich Hegel and August Schilling, without success. However, the more "incomprehensible" he found these writings the more "he felt desirous of probing the question of the 'absolute' and everything connected therewith to the core." In the end, as he put it, "I always returned to the Ninth Symphony."[54]

Feuerbach's concepts of the "importance of feeling" and getting in touch with the unconscious resonated with Wagner, who, in his quest for the absolute, was far more impacted by the mysticism of the Ninth Symphony than by any philosophical reasonings.

Feuerbach writes, and "Wagner reads, "Human feelings...have ontological and metaphysical significance. In feelings – indeed, in the feelings of daily occurrence – the deepest and highest truths are concealed...the new philosophy rests on the truth of love and feeling...the new philosophy itself is basically nothing other than the essence of feeling elevated to consciousness."(55)

Wagner dedicated his essay *The Art Work of the Future* published in 1849, to Feuerbach and writes "In the drama we become knowers through feeling. Things which can be explained by the infinite accommodations of the intellect are incomprehensible and disturbing to the feeling."(56)

Two years later in Opera and Drama he writes "the poet can dispense with any aid from the mechanism of logic and address himself with full consciousness to the infallible recapture process of the unconscious, purely human feeling."(57)

Let's go back to Webster's definition of mysticism..." the possibility of the spiritual apprehension of knowledge inaccessible to the intellect." Wagner is on a mystical bent and writes that it is his orchestra which "will provide the soil of infinite universal feeling."

In the *The Philosophy of the Future*, Feuerbach also stressed the importance of love. "Love is objectively as well as subjectively the criterion of being, of truth and of reality, where there is no love, there also is no truth. And only in he who loves something is something; to be nothing and to love nothing are identical. The more one is, the more one loves, and vice versa...The new philosophy recognizes the truth of sensation with joy and consciousness; it's the open-hearted and sensuous philosophy."(58)

Freidrich Engels wrote, "The enthusiasm [about Feuerbach] was universal. We were all, for the time being, Feuerbachians."(59) Karl Marx in *The Holy Family* wrote "Feuerbach's extravagant glorification of love which when compared with the insufferable sovereignty of pure reason, was easy to excuse if not to justify."(60)

These thoughts found their way into the *Ring* which, in simplified terms, deals with the love of power changing to the power of love.

The repressive love of power personified by Wotan and Alberich is superceded by the power of Brunhilde's love of humanity, and the solution to the Ring's conflict becomes a metaphysical one rather than a political one.

Feuerbach's philosophy was an optimistic philosophy, and he saw history as progressive. Both Feuerbach and Wagner had a positive view of mankind, a noble-savage type of optimism. Wagner shared Feuerbach's view that this was at odds with the teachings of the Catholic Church which had degraded mankind. In the essay *Art and Revolution* published in 1849, Wagner writes:

"Christianity adjusts the ills of an honourless, useless, and sorrowful existence of mankind on earth, by the miraculous love of God, who had not as the noble Greeks supposed – a created man for a happy and self-conscious life upon this earth, but had imprisoned him in a loathsome dungeon: so as, in reward for the self-contempt that poisoned him therein, to prepare him for a posthumous state of endless comfort and inactive ecstasy."[61]

As mentioned before, Wagner continued his study of religions all his life. In 1852, he discovered Hafiz, a fourteenth century Sufi mystic and poet. *The Divan*, by Hafiz, had recently been translated into German, and Wagner found some of his own thinking in its poetry. On September 12, 1852, Wagner wrote to his friend, August Röeckel, who was still imprisoned as a result of his participation with Wagner in the Dresden uprisings of 1849, as follows:

"I would also introduce you to a poet whom I have recently recognized to be the greatest of all poets; it is the Persian poet Hafiz. Familiarity with this poet has filled me with a very sense of terror; we with our pompous European intellectual culture must stand abashed in the presence of this product of the Orient, with its self assurance and sub-

lime tranquility of mind...I like to see in the person of this
Oriental a precocious striving after individualism."(62)

While writing *Jesus of Nazareth*, Wagner had written to his
friend, Theodore Uhlig, of his own individualism: "Whoever satisfies
the inner necessity of his being is free; because he feels himself at one
with himself, because everything which he does answers to his nature,
to his true needs."(63)

In *The Divan*, Hafiz also expressed the belief that the union of
our own souls with God was possible and required only that we seek
the answer within – the same metaphysical and mystical thought
expressed by Wagner in *Jesus of Nazareth*. Later, Wagner encountered
similar thoughts while studying Hinduism and Buddhism.

CHAPTER FIVE

SCHOPENHAUER

In November of 1853 Wagner resumed composing, but, as usual, he continued reading and sorting out his own ideas. Towards the end of 1854, his friend, George Herwegh, introduced him to the writings of the German philosopher, Arthur Schopenhauer. It would have a great impact on his thinking and his life. Ernest Newman in his classic four volume biography of Wagner writes that the impact of Schopenhauer on Wagner "was the most powerful thing of the kind that his mind had ever had or was afterwards to know."(64)

Thomas Mann writes in his essay *Sufferings and Greatness of Richard Wagner* "the acquaintance with the philosophy of Arthur Schopenhauer was the greatest event in Wagner's life. No earlier intellectual contact, such as that with Feuerbach, approaches it in personal and historical significance. It meant to him the deepest consolation, the highest self-confirmation; it meant the release of mind and spirit, it was utterly the right thing."(65)

Most importantly, Schopenhauer helped Wagner understand himself, as Thomas Mann said, "the highest self-confirmation". Writing to Röeckel August 23, 1856, Wagner said, "I must confess to having arrived at a clear understanding of my own works through the help of another, who provided me with the reasoned conceptions corresponding to my intuitive principles."(66) This is a very important point. Much of Schopenhauer's thinking Wagner had already developed intuitively if not cognitively.

Wagner read Schopenhauer's *The World as Will and Representation* four times in three months and reread it many times in the years to come. Wagner not only read it, he understood it. Nietzsche attested to that fact, and Nietzsche certainly qualified as a judge of that understanding. Wagner was so taken by this book, that until the end of his life – he sought out anybody who would sit and listen to him expound on Schopenhauer. Actually, Wagner did a better job of promoting Schopenhauer than Schopenhauer ever did.

There are many areas in which Schopenhauer is said to have impacted Wagner. Several of them have mystical implications.

Schopenhauer is known as the philosopher of pessimism, and in my view, too much emphasis has been put on Schopenhauer causing Wagner to take a pessimistic view of things. Wagner himself is responsible for this. In his letter to Röeckel of August 23, 1856, Wagner says that after reading Schopenhauer he realized that unconsciously he was taking a different path in the *Ring* than one he originally had intended, changing from "an optimistic view of the world based on Hellenic principles, to a pessimistic one recognizing the nothingness of the world."[67]

In the eight years between 1848 when Wagner published the first prose draft of his *Ring of the Nibelung* and 1856 when Wagner wrote Röeckel, Wagner's conception of the *Ring* was changing, and he continuously struggled to find the right words for the final scene. In the original ending conceived by Wagner in 1848 during his revolutionary or optimistic period, Wotan and the Gods continued to reign redeemed by Seigfried's death and Brunnhilde's immolation.

In 1851 Wagner changed the ending. The Gods pass away as Wotan had willed it and receive "blessed death redemption."

In 1852 Wagner added an element of the importance of love. As Andrew Porter describes it, "the quest for wealth and power can never produce a happy world, only love can bestow the blessing that this world needs."[68] This is generally referred to as the "Feuerbach ending" because of its emphasis on love.

After reading *The World as Will and Idea* and the books on eastern religions and Buddhism that Schopenhauer recommended, Wagner conceived a new ending to *Götterdammerung*. The basic elements remained the same with the Gods perishing, but Brunnhilde reaches a new level of enlightenment and the Buddhistic concept of metampsychosis (reincarnation) is introduced. She sings that by her immolation she is "going to the desire-free illusion-free holiest chosen land, the goal of world wandering, released from rebirth", and adds "The blessed end of all things are eternal, do you know how I attained it? Deepest suffering of grieving love opened my eyes; I saw the world end."

This so-called "Schopenhaurian ending" was replaced with the ending which has been used ever since with the Gods perishing, the Ring being returned to the Rhine, and Brunnhilde, in her immolation, greeting Siegfried as his wife. However, the "Schopenhaurian ending" which Deryck Cooke in *I Saw the World End* describes as "expressing renunciation of the material world as an illusion, and a dissolution into a state of non-being" (surely a mystical state) was never completely abandoned by Wagner. He added it as a footnote to the final text with a comment that it had fallen out because "its meaning was already expressed with the greatest precision" in the music.

What does this all mean? And what is the significance of the humans who come out on the stage at the final curtain witnessing the destruction of Valhalla and the Gods? Is this the end of the world? Is there a new and better world replacing the old? Röeckel had written to Wagner for an explanation as to "Why, since the Rhinegold is restored to the Rhine, the Gods still perish?" Wagner admitted that he was unable to find the right words for the ending and that Röeckel (and we) had to listen to the music to find the answer. He wrote:

> "I have now come to realize again how much there is, owing to the whole nature of my poetic aim, that only becomes clear through the music. I now simply cannot look at the uncomposed poem any more."[69]

This must have been very frustrating for Wagner who considered himself as a poet first and a musician second, and in his writings generally spoke of the poet rather than the musician or the composer.

Wagner does try to explain his inability to articulate the ineffable in the final ending of the Ring by saying "How can a composer have his intuitive perceptions understood by others, when he himself stands before an enigma, and can suffer the same illusions as everyone else?"(70) No doubt he was acquainted with the words of his idol, Goethe, that "the more incommensurable, and the more incomprehensible to the understanding, a poetic production is, the better it is."(71)

Perhaps another favorite of Wagner, George Gordon Lord Byron, said it best in his *Child Harold's Pilgrimage:* "To mingle with the universe and feel, what I cannot express yet cannot all conceal."

In a mystical way Wagner's own music spoke to Wagner himself. While composing *Siegfried* in December of 1856 Wagner wrote to Liszt:

"It's strange! It's only now that that I am composing
that the true essence of my text is being revealed to me:
everywhere I am discovering secrets which until now
have remained hidden even from me."(72)

In light of all this, it's best to take Wagner's advice and consult the music at the end of *Götterdammerung* for the meaning. The last motif played is the one generally referred to as "redemption through love", although Wagner referred to it as the "Glorification of Brunnhilde". This motif appears only one other time in the *Ring*, in *Die Walkure* when Sieglinde is told that she is going to bear Siegmund's child and that his name will be Siegfried. The music there expresses ecstasy and hope for the future. When it reappears at the end of *Götterdammerung*, it is much more serene – a type of epiphany. The feeling it evokes here can best be described as "blessedness and peace."

Deryck Cooke had it right in *I Saw the World End*, that in the years of composition of the *Ring* libretto, Wagner had changed from a political solution in the *Ring*, to a metaphysical one; and although Wagner, and we as well, found it to be ineffable, the feeling (remember, we become knowers through feeling)...one of blessedness and peace... is certainly not a pessimistic one. For that matter, none of the operas

Wagner completed after reading Schopenhauer in 1854 have a pessimistic resolution – *Götterdammerung, Tristan, Die Meistersinger,* or *Parsifal*...and the final chords of *Tristan* and *Parsifal*, like *Götterdammerung*, evoke a feeling of blessedness and peace.

The fact is that most of Schopenhauer's philosophy is compatible with an optimistic point of view, and that is particularly true of the areas which most influenced Wagner, Schopenhauer's metaphysics and his aesthetics.

Feuerbach's concepts of the importance of feeling and of raising man's unconscious to the level conscious had helped Wagner with his efforts to develop his own metaphysics, but Schopenhauer took this much further. Wagner writes in his autobiography, "what fascinated me so enormously about Schopenhauer's work was not only its extraordinary fate, but the clearness and manly precision with which the most difficult metaphysical problems were treated from the very beginning."[73]

In his metaphysics Schopenhauer picked up where Emmanual Kant left off. Schopenhauer felt that Plato and Kant were by far the greatest philosophers who ever lived and that nothing philosophically important had happened after Plato, until Kant came along. Kant took Plato's ideas of the world's eternal forms and added a very important ingredient which Schopenhauer thought was a stroke of genius. That is, he explained why you cannot ever get to know the world of eternal forms. The reason is that we are restricted by the apparatus that we have in our body. We can only see and hear and smell and so forth. Being restricted by this, we can only be in touch with the world reached by our senses, which is the phenomenal world.

But Kant said there also is a noumenal world, similar to Plato's world of eternal forms. Kant called them "things-in-themselves" rather than eternal forms, and this world is unknowable to the individual.

Schopenhauer took this idea and said that, there is a phenomenal world, the world that we know through our senses, and another world of eternal forms, but that world is not the noumenal world. The noumenal world is a world above all that. And whereas the eternal forms and Kant's things-in-themselves, have a multiplicity of things in them, the noumenal world of Schopenhauer is made of *one* substance, and only one, and that is "Will," which we cannot really ever get to know. The closest we ever come to knowing the noumenal world of Will is in the act of making love or by creating, performing or listening to music. That certainly must have appealed to Wagner! He interrupted his composition of the *Ring* to compose two operas, one celebrating love, *Tristan*, and the other celebrating music, *Die Meistersinger*.

As for his aesthetics, Schopenhauer said that there is a hierarchy of the arts. He felt that one could be in touch with the eternal forms of the world — the middle world between the phenomenal and the noumenal — through architecture, sculpture, and painting. A genius was someone who sees the universal in the particular...a Wagnerian thought. The genius artist is one who can convey his sense of the universal to the person viewing the painting, so that person feels the same thing that the artist feels...another Wagnerian thought.

Schopenhauer goes on to describe the nature of genius. "The typical genius has an unusually strong imagination...a vitality with restless ambition; that ceaseless desire for new things and for the contemplation of enobling things...a longing seldom satisfied for peoples of like mind with whom he might communicate. He is often subject to violent emotions and irrational passions."(74) In reading this, Wagner must have thought, "He's talking about me!"

Schopenhauer said that the highest of all arts was music, and that music conveys to the listener what nothing else can convey. He referred to music as the "voice of the noumenal".

"Music is so much more powerful and penetrating than the other arts, for they speak only of the shadow, while music speaks of the essence...Suitable music played to any scene, activity, event or circumstance, seems to divulge the most secret meaning of that occasion."(75)

Schopenhauer goes on to say:

"Music does not express this or that particular and definite pleasure, this or that affection, pain, sorrow, horror, gaiety, merriment or peace of mind, but joy, pain, sorrow, horror, gaiety, merriment peace of mind themselves."[76]

Compare these words to those that Wagner used in 1848 at age 35. "What music expresses is eternal, infinite and ideal. It speaks none of the passion, love, and longing of this or that individual in this or that situation, but of passion, love and longing in themselves." You can see that when Wagner picked up this book and read it, he felt that he was having a conversation with himself.

Schopenhauer also deals with bringing the unconscious to conscious and becoming knowers through feeling – a two important elements of the Wagner fabric. "Let us compare our consciousness to the sheet of water of some depth. The distinctly conscious ideas are merely surface. On the other hand, the mass of the water is the indistinct, the feelings, the after sensation of perceptions and intuitions and what is experienced in general. Hence, we often are unable to give any account of the origin of our deepest thoughts. They are the offspring of a mysterious inner being. Judgments, sudden flashes of thought, resolves, rise from the depths unexpectedly, to our own astonishment. Consciousness is the mere surface of our mind, and of this, as of the globe, we do not know the interior but only the crust."[77]

To Schopenhauer, music is the voice of the noumena speaking to the listener. He writes, "Music is an unconscious exercise in metaphysics, in which the mind does not know that it's philosophizing. The composer reveals the innermost essence of the world and expresses the deepest wisdom in a language that his reason does not understand...in the same way a person mesmerized talks about things of which he had no idea of when awake."[78]

It's easy to see the kinship that Wagner felt with Schopenhauer particularly in the areas of metaphysics and aesthetics. As well as a revelation to Wagner of his unconscious or intuitive thoughts, it was a confirmation of ideas he already had developed cognitively. Bryan Magee in the *Tristan Chord*, apparently sees in the unconscious to the conscious process and the euphoria that Wagner felt as a result, a similarity with what happens to us when listening to Wagner's music: "Schopenhauer put Wagner in touch with his own unconscious. As this is the key to what Wagner, himself, does for those who are susceptible to his art, it explains why Wagner's attitude of adulation for Schopenhauer is similar to our attitude towards Wagner."(79)

CHAPTER SIX

TRISTAN

Shortly after his first reading of *The World as Will and Idea*, in 1854, Wagner wrote to Franz Liszt of his intention to compose a new opera based on the Tristan and Isolde legend.

"While I had never in my life enjoyed true happiness of love, I intend to erect a further monument to this most beautiful of dreams, a monument in which this love will for once be thoroughly satiated from beginning to end: I have planned in my head a *Tristan and Isolde*, the simplest but most beautiful full blooded musical composition; with the "black flag" which flutters at the end. I shall then cover myself in order to die."[80]

When he finally got around to the composition of the music for the new opera, he flung himself into the task, and the music seemed to pour out of him. Jeffrey Swann, the concert pianist and musicologist, who has studied the original score, says that the music seems "to swim on the page as if Wagner couldn't put the notes down fast enough."[81]

The result was Wagner's most mystical work to that date – a musical expression of Schopenhauer's idea that life is a continual striving and longing which can never be fully satisfied, and that release can only come through death.

Day becomes the symbol of the phenomenal world, and night becomes the symbol of the noumenal world. Although I can find no mention in Wagner's writings of his reading Novalis at this time, much of the language found in this French romantic poet's "Hymn to the Night" turns up in Wagner's libretto during the second act love duet.

Tristan and Isolde here are singing metaphysics. The eminent Wagner authority, Michael Tanner, points out that "when Tristan arrives after the first minutes of incoherent rapture, the lovers are accompanied by the most intoxicatingly sensual music Wagner ever wrote, embark on an elaborate dialectic, in which they contrast, with incredible intellectual zest, considering how aroused they are, Night and Day, Love and Death, Betrayal and Loyalty, and their own names in each case shifting the balance of their approvals from one to the other, until at the climax of the middle section of the duet, to the accompaniment of the orchestra rocking them on metaphysical waves, they join in singing 'selbt dann bin ich die Welt' ('then I myself am the world'). Their individualities have disappeared with the daylight, which they equate with appearance, custom, chivalry and that kind of superficiality, and now they are servants of Night, knowing that there are no separate selves, that indeed they are everything."[82]

This, of course, is what Walter T. Stace calls "the nuclear and essential characteristic of all metaphysical experience when personal identity is lost and one is merged or dissolved in an infinite or universal ocean of being."

Schopenhauer himself supplied the musical means to express the extreme striving and longing by the use of the suspension, "a dissonance delaying the final consonance that is certainly awaited; in this way the longing for it is strengthened, and its appearance affords the greater satisfaction. This is clearly an analogue of the satisfaction of the will which is enhanced through delay."[83] Wagner's continuous use of this device for five or so hours keeps the audience entranced and leaves them virtually exhausted at the end with the final resolution.

It is important to note that whereas the music of *Tristan* has been described as the most sensuous music ever composed, and some critics have labeled passages in the second act as musical orgasms, the union which Tristan and Isolde seek is a mystical union not a physical one.

Jeffrey Swann in his lecture, *Tristan and the Mystic Experience*, points out that unlike most operas in which the audience is caught up with learning about the story, "*Tristan* is really about itself – the experience of hearing it. It is an exploration of the realm of death or in part, of limitless infinity, timelessness, a sense of longing for eternity, and makes us live this experience. This is a mystic experience in that you experience it as something you live rather than think about or learn."[84] Thus it is Wagner's music rather than his words, that enables listeners to live a mystic experience of "oneness" when Tristan and Isolde sing "then I myself am the world."

Michael Tanner feels that *Tristan* is a religious work in that it evokes a religious feeling and along with Bach's *St. Matthew Passion*, is one of the greatest religious works of our culture. He writes:

> "The experience of love at its most intense becomes an intuition that its fulfillment can only be found in a reincarnation of the self...It is the seriousness with which Wagner expresses and explores that intuition that leads me to say that in the end Tristan is a religious work."[85]

The "reincarnation of the self" here is similar to Wagner's "divestment of me" as expressed in *Jesus of Nazareth*.

Tanner goes on to say:

> *Tristan...* is an impossible achievement. We worship it partly because we are unable to understand it; that is another of its qualifications for religious status. Wagner judged to a T the degree to which, in order to found a new religion, it was necessary to make it incomprehensible.[86]

Ernest Newman writes: "That mystical abstraction from the real world that we find *Tristan and Isolde* trying to give expression to was merely the sublimation of a frame of mind that was quite common to Wagner"[87]

But Wagner was aware that the intensity of the mystical feelings he was having when composing the music to *Tristan* would be felt by his audience with the potential for serious consequences. In a brief but feverish note he wrote to Matilda Wessendonk in April of 1859 Wagner wrote:

"Child! The Tristan is turning into something *dreadful*.
"That last Act!!!-----
"I'm afraid the opera will be forbidden – unless the
   whole thing is turned into a parody by bad pro-
   duction-----; only mediocre performances can save
   me! Completely good ones are bound to drive
   people crazy – I can't imagine what else could
   happen. To such a state have things come!!!
Alas!-----
I was just going full steam ahead!
Adieu"[88]

Later in August of 1860, he wrote again to her:
   Upon reading it through again, I couldn't believe
   my eyes or ears. How terribly I shall have to pay for this
   work some day if I intend to see it performed I *distinctly
   foresee the most unheard-of sufferings*; for in it – I can't hide
   the fact – I've over-stepped whatever lies within the
   power of execution.[89]

Wagner's concerns seem to have been warranted. The first Tristan,
Aloys Ander, declared the work impossible after numerous rehearsals
and died insane before the first performance.

The Tristan at the first performance in 1865, Ludwig Schnorr von
Carolsfeld, died suddenly after singing it. The Isolde – Schnorr's wife
Malvina, turned to spiritualism and later died insane.

Schnorr had been one of Wagner's favorite singers, and Wagner
felt that somehow he had sacrificed himself to the opera. Wagner's
diary reads:
   "My Tristan! My Beloved! I drove you to the abyss...
   I lay hold of him to check him, to draw him back, and
   I push him over...And myself? My head does not swim,
   I look down: it even delights me, But – the friend? Him
   I lose! Mein Tristan! Mein Trauter!"[90]

The conductor of *Tristan*, Hans von Bullow, wrote:

> "*Tristan* has given me the *coup de grace*...Poor Eberle, Richter's pet répétiteur, was driven mad during the rehearsals by the opera-itself (we tell the public it was an excess of beer); as for me, who confess always to have lacked the necessary courage in my numerous arrangements for taking my life, I assure you I could not have resisted the temptation if anyone had offered me a few drops of prussic acid."(91)

In attending a performance at Bayreuth in 1886, Franz Liszt suffered a heart attack during the second act and a second one in the third act when the same notes were repeated that were being played when he had the first attack. This attack proved to be fatal, and when he died two days later his last word, according to his daughter, Cosima, was "Tristan!"

In 1889 the French composers, César Franck and Ernest Chausson together with a young student, attended their first *Tristan*, at Bayreuth. The student was emotionally overcome after the Prelude and had to leave. Chausson left sobbing during the second act, and Franck didn't make it through the last act.

These are just a few of the anecdotal stories of the mysterious impact of the *Tristan* music that have developed over the years. Many were recalled when the 2008 season Metropolitan Opera production went through four tenors, and the Met's 2009 production went through two tenors and three Isoldes.

CHAPTER SEVEN

EASTERN INFLUENCES

Sometime after Schopenhauer had formulated his philosophy he discovered to his amazement that many of his principal concepts were very similar to those developed and written about centuries before by Eastern religion mystics. They included (1) that the world we experience is limited by our senses and is a world of appearances only; (2) that contrary to these appearances the world is basically one; (3) that any sense of our being part of that one is ineffable, and (4) that the oneness explains our feeling of compassion for others.

Schopenhauer became a student of Hinduism and Buddhism, read profusely about them, and recommended that others do the same. As a result, Wagner acquired and read several of these books including a translation of *The Upanishads*, ancient accounts of Hindu mystical revelations, and Eugene Bernouf's *Introduction a L'histoire du Bouddhisme*, along with the writings of Meister Eckhart, a 13th century Christian mystic also recommended by Schopenhauer.

Just as Schopenhauer did, Wagner discovered many of his own ideas expressed in these centuries old mystical writings.

The concept of discovering God within the individual expressed in *Jesus of Nazareth* – "I bring man back into himself in that he apprehendeth God in himself and not outside him" is expressed in The Upanishads – "The secret of immortality is to be found...in realization of the identity of the Self within and Brahman without, for immortality is union with God."(92) Meister Eckhart writes "The eye for which I see God is the same eye which God sees me."(93)

The loss of individualization while at the same time becoming one with something universal is expressed in *Jesus of Nazareth* as the "divestment of the Me" and "and an ascent into the generality." *The Upanishads* say "Beyond the senses...is pure unitary conscious, where awareness of the world and of multiplicity is completely obliterated. It is ineffable peace. It is the supreme good. It is One without a second."(94) Meister Eckhart describes this as "nothing can disturb or diversify this man who is one in *The One* where all multiplicity is one and homogenous."(95)

Wagner and Meister Eckhart agree that God can be discovered within the self without the need to attend church. In *Jesus of Nazareth*, Jesus says "No longer do you think to serve God by going to the temple" while Meister Eckhart writes "to seek God in rituals is to get the ritual and lose God in the process."(96)

Like Schopenhauer, Wagner and Cosima continued to read the *The Upanishads* as the years rolled by. Cosima writes in her diaries: "In the evening played Beethoven quartets with Richard; the composure of the heart spoken of in *The Upanishads* is thus miraculously attained, and on this composure a *ringing* delight floats as on clear, still water. Here is *Brahman*, devoutness achieved, this is nonexistence and one is close to the All-Seeing."(97)

They also continued to read and to discuss the writings of Meister Eckhart and his student, the mystic Johannes Tauler. In laying out the religious education of their son, Siegfried, they said that it should be restricted to the readings and teachings of Eckhart and Tauler.

There are many references in Cosima's diary concerning Wagner's interest in mysticism. They discussed the writings of Jacob Boehm (1575-1625), a German mystic who like Hans Sachs, was a cobbler. In March of 1873, Cosima also notes "Richard is pleased with his books, particularly with the new arrived mystics." She quotes Wagner as saying, "The mystic is the man for me, even if he is mistaken – the man who feels the urge to ignite for himself the inner light in contrast to the outer brightness which shows him nothing; the name *Illuminati* was for this reason aptly chosen."(98)

Over the centuries many mystic organizations adopted the name "Illuminati". Supposedly of Gnostic origin, they claimed that they experienced a "light" that was communicated from a higher source or as due to a clarified and exalted condition of intelligence. The Rosicrucians, a secret society which originated in the fifteenth century, adopted the name and attracted a number of literary figures including Goethe whom Wagner revered. The Bavarian government ruled them illegal in 1785, but many Germans, including Wagner, maintained an interest in their ideas.

The inner light was one of Wagner's favorite concepts, often referring to it with religious connotations. In his *On State and Religion* he wrote:

> "This is the essence of true religion...it shines in the
> night of man's inmost heart with a light quite other
> than the world-sun light and visible nowhere save from
> out that depth."[99]

It is clear that in the development of his own metaphysical thinking Wagner developed a belief in mysticism. He preferred the Eastern mystics to the Western ones and expressed this in a letter to Matilda Wessendonk in April of 1864:

> "I have the German Christian mystics in front of me;
> today it is Tauler. The entry of 'grace' is always deeply
> affecting. Nonetheless, everything on the Ganges is
> more expansive, more peaceful, and more serene than in
> the cells of these Christian monks."[100]

He had written to Liszt that "modern research has succeeded in showing that pure and unalloyed Christianity was nothing but a branch of the venerable Buddhism which, after Alexander's Indian expeditions spread to the shores of the Mediteranean."[101]

Wagner was in tune with thoughts expressed in the Hindu Upanishads:

> "As a lump of salt thrown into water melts away...
> even so, the individual soul, dissolved in the Eternal –
> pure consciousness, infinite transcendent."[102]

And by Schopenhauer's:

> We are one with the world and therefore not oppressed, but exalted in its immensity. It is the consciousness of this and that the Upanishads of the Vedas express again and again, formulating it in different ways, but most admirably in the saying 'I am all these creatures, and besides me there is no other being'. It is the transcending of our own individual self, the sense of the sublime.[103]

In addition to the books on Hinduism and Buddhism which he had accumulated and read thanks to Schopenhauer's recommendations, Wagner had a statue of the Buddha installed at Wahnfried, his house in Bayreuth.

His intimate friend, Count de Gobineau, wrote that "Wagner was a Buddhist in his heart, and called himself so." In writing to a friend in Paris in 1859 Wagner signed the letter "your grateful Buddhist."[104]

In 1856 Wagner decided to compose a new opera called *Die Sieger* (*The Victors*) based on a Buddhist legend found in Burnouf's *Introduction a L'Histoire du Bouddhisme*. Paul Schofield, a former Buddhist monk, explains in his book *The Redeemer Born*, "that the term 'victor' is used here in the Buddhist context to refer to those who have been victorious in the quest for enlightenment."[105] In the story, Prakiti, an Indian maiden, "falls in love with Ananda, knowing that he is a celebate monk and therefore unavailable for marriage." Prakiti goes to the Buddha to ask him what she can do. Knowing that Prakiti had misbehaved in a former life, he tells her "that she can expiate her former actions and find full redemption by entering his monastic order." Here she "finds true love in the spiritual sense, not in the romantic sense" and is united with Ananda spiritually finding eternal life through union with the noumenon.

Wagner worked on *Die Sieger* off and on for twenty years, even composing some of the music, although he eventually abandoned the project, feeling that the real message of *Die Sieger*, the path to enlightenment, was finding its way into *Parsifal*. The music that he composed as a leit motif for the Buddha turns up in *Siegfried* and in *Götterdamerung* and has become known as "the world inheritance" motif, although it is interesting that Wagner called it the "renunciation" motif, (Erlœsungmotif). Heinrich Porges in his *Wagner Rehearsing the Ring* describes the importance that Wagner gave this music when it first appears in Siegfried:

> Wagner expressly demanded that the *Redemption* theme as it enters after Wotan's words, "Was in des Zwiespalt's wildem Schmerze verweifelnd eins ich beschloss, froh und fredig führe, frei ich nun aus"…(what is my spirit's fiercest anguish despairing once I resolved, glad and blithesome – freshly I bring on now to pass) should be taken 'slightly faster' than the preceding bars and that it should be 'very brought out' (sehr heraus), as he tersely put it. He once characterised the spiritual significance of this theme (whilst still going on through the work at the piano) by the statement: 'It must sound like the proclamation of a new religion'…Taken a shade faster the effect of the sudden illumination by which Wotan himself is overwhelmed is all the more powerful…Subsequently the performance of the whole scene must be imbued by this revelation of spiritual renewal.[106]

Note the use of the words "sudden illumination" reminiscent of the *"scientia visionis"* in Plato's *Symposium*.

In a letter to Matilda Wessendonk dated October 5, 1858, Wagner spoke about his musical treatment of the Buddha:

> The difficulty here was to make the Buddha himself – a figure totally liberated and above all passion – suitable for dramatic and, more especially, musical treatment. But I have now solved the problem by having him

reach one last remaining stage in his development whereby he is seen to acquire a new insight, which – like every insight – is conveyed not by the abstract associations of ideas but by intuitive emotional experience, in other words, by a process of shock and agitation suffered by his inner self; as a result, this insight reveals him in his progress towards a state of supreme enlightenment.[107]

Earlier in April of 1856 Wagner had written to Roeckel: "We cannot accept a thing cognitively if we have not grasped it intuitively."[108] Here Wagner defines "grasp it intuitively" as an insight conveyed by an intuitive emotional experience, a process of shock and agitation suffered by his inner self "leading to supreme enlightenment."

It is this path to supreme enlightenment which Wagner takes up in *Parsifal*. It is based on the Buddhistic concept *Bodhisattva*, one who reaches total enlightenment by growing in wisdom and compassion, each enhancing the other. Thus in *Parsifal*, Wagner gave the grail legend a decidedly eastern flavor. *Parsifal* grows in wisdom and compassion to spiritual enlightenment, and it is Kundry's kiss that provides the sudden shock and agitation.

In describing the moment to King Ludwig Wagner wrote about Parsifal "a tremendous remembrance of fellow-suffering arose from deep within him, sounding its shrill lament; now he knows."[109]

Mitleid, or compassion, was the central theme of the ethics of the Buddhists, Schopenhauer and Wagner. It is a mysterious thing that when one sees another suffering one feels that suffering himself and the greater the suffering, the greater the compassion. Schopenhauer explains this mystery as a natural result of his metaphysics. Since we are all one within the noumenal, we have a natural kinship with others.

Wagner along with the Buddhists thought that this had to be attained – a progression through wisdom and compassion. Furthermore, he felt that this was the path to redemption. In a letter to Roeckel in 1855 he wrote:

"through this knowledge...we attain to a sympathy
with all things living...In this perfect unison which
has been kept apart from us by the illusion of indi-
viduation lies the root of all virtue, the true secret
of redemption."(110)

It is a mystical thought akin to the "abandonment of the self" and
the ascent into the generality" that Wagner expressed in *Jesus of
Nazareth*. Thus *Parsifal* ends with the chorus singing "Redeemed,
our Redeemer".

Parsifal had been on Wagner's mind ever since reading Wolfram von
Eschenbach's Parsifal at Marienbad in 1845. In 1857 while composing
Tristan he thought of composing an opera on the subject sensing con-
sciously or unconsciously that it fit very well into the Schopenhauerian
and Buddhistic thoughts he had at the time. As he read other versions
of the story he developed thoughts as to how to put his own Wagnerian
spin on the tale, but this was to be an important work, and his thoughts
had to mature.

In 1860 he wrote to Mathilde Wesendonk:

"Parzival is again very much coming to life in me;
all the time I see it more and more clearly; when one
day it is all finally ripe in me, the bringing of this poem
into the world will be for me an extreme pleasure. But
between now and then a good few years may yet have to
pass...I shall put it off as long as I can, and I concern
myself with it only when it forces me to. But then this
extraordinary process of generation does let me forget
all my troubles."(111)

He felt that this was to be his last work and said so in letters to
Mathilde Maier in 1864 and to Wendelin Weissheimer in 1862. He also
referred to *Parsifal* "as my farewell to the world."(112)

In order to achieve the mystical other-worldliness he wanted for the
work, a special type of theater was required, and the Festspielhaus in

Bayreuth provided just that. *Parsifal* was the only opera composed by Wagner after the erection of that theater.

The orchestral cover at Bayreuth not only focused the audience's full attention on what was happening on the stage, but also brought the audience closer to the singers while creating Wagner's own version of surround sound. Significantly he called this "the mystical abyss". It worked! After the first performance in 1882 Wagner wrote:

> The influence of our surrounding optic and acoustic atmosphere bore our souls away from the wonted world; and the consciousness of this was evident in our dread at the thought of going back into that world. Yes, 'Parsifal' itself had owned its origin and evolution to escape therefrom![113]

Of all Wagner's operas, *Tristan* and *Parsifal* are the most mystical. The prelude to *Parsifal* has a mystical quality similar to that of the prelude of *Lohengrin*; of course, both operas deal with the Grail. As Jules Cashford wrote in *The Household of the Grail Tradition*: "The Grail prepares us for a passage beyond the known bounds and form of space, time and causality. It remains a vision where time and eternity are at one."[114]

The musicologist, Saul Lilienstein, in his *CD Commentary on Parsifal*, describes his reaction to the opening measures of the Prelude as follows: Where are we? This plaintive melody moving along on its way without the benefit of classical balance...the tonality ambiguous...and the very time of it seeming to be suspended...Where for the love of God are we?"[115] From the very beginning, Wagner has established that we are in a mystical world outside the phenomenal world of time and space.

As early as 1851 in *Opera and Drama*, Wagner had written:

> To set the unity of the Drama within the unity of Space and Time, means to set it at *naught*; for Time and Space are nothing in themselves, and only become

something through their being *annulled* by something real...Time and Space are annhilated through the actuality of the Drama."(116)

While composing *Parsifal*, Wagner was still involved with his readings of the Eastern mystics and was very well acquainted with two of its most important thoughts, the basic oneness of the world and the indivisibility of space and time. Wagner expresses the latter concept where Gürnemanz tells Parsifal in Act One, "Here time and space are indivisible."

The Wagnerian authority Robert Bailey of New York University received a letter from a scientist at the National Academy of Science, referring to Gürnemanz's comment, inquiring as to whether it was possible that a German operatic composer had expressed Einstein's theory of relativity years before Einstein was born. What he did not know was that the Eastern mystics had intuitively "discovered" both Einstein's theory and the basic concept of quantum physics, that all matter is made of one substance, centuries before Western scientists discovered them rationally and that the well read composer, Wagner, had embraced these thoughts and was well aware of what he was doing. Cosima's diary of December 21, 1877, quotes Wagner: "Today I have set a philosophical precept to music: 'Hence space becomes time.'"

Perhaps it was the Persian mystical poet Hafiz who, in 1852, first turned Wagner's interest towards the east. If so, it was to have a lasting impact on him.

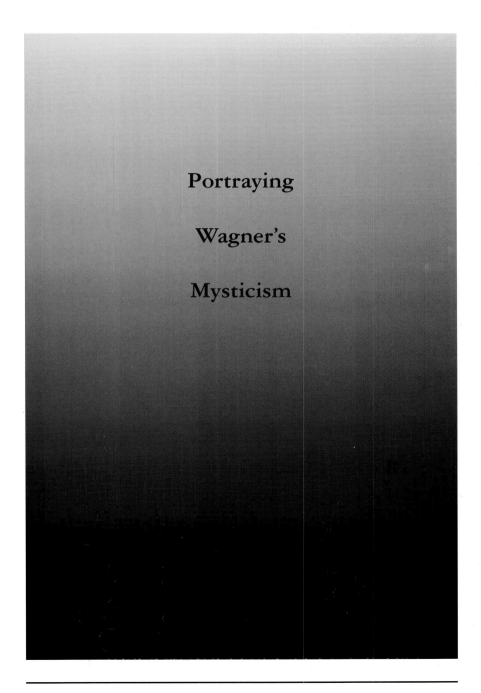

Portraying

Wagner's

Mysticism

Portraying Wagner's Mysticism

The visual representation of Wagner's music dramas was, and continues to be, a real challenge. Richard Wagner had definite thoughts as to how his music dramas should be staged, true to the mythological and mystical content of his work. He had said that if they could not be presented as he intended, they should not be performed at all. He wrote detailed and extensive stage directions for the singers and hired the best artists available to paint scenery. His many innovations included magic lantern projections to portray Valkyries on their horses for the Ride of the Valkyries scene.

Handling the elaborate scene changes and finding singers who could both sing and act competently proved to be a difficult task. In her diary entry of September 23, 1878, Cosima quotes Wagner's frustration with getting the staging right: "Having created the invisible orchestra, I now feel like inventing the invisible theatre!"

The same year, writing in *The Public in Time and Space*, Wagner seems to have anticipated what directors might some day do to his music dramas: "Almost every operatic regisseur has at some time attempted to trim *Don Giovanni* to the day; whereas every intelligent person should reflect that not this work must be altered to fit our times, but ourselves to the times of *Don Giovanni*, if we are to arrive at harmony with Mozart's creation."

Today most European, and many American productions take a revisionist approach bent on finding new ways to "interpret" Wagner, often resulting in stagings that are hardly recognizable as being Wagnerian were it not for the music.

A handful of productions have taken a more traditional approach to staging Wagner's operas while utilizing modern technical advances in stage-craft and employing theatre-seasoned directors consistent with Wagner's original intentions. These productions such as Speight

Jenkins' Seattle *Ring* and Günther Schneider-Siemssen's *Ring* and *Parsifal* at the Metropolitan Opera have attracted many attendees from Europe who were unable to find anything "traditional" in their homelands.

Over the years some of the most effective visual presentations capturing some of the mysticism of Wagner's operas can be found in the works of artists such as Henri Fantin-Letour, Arthur Rackham, and Ul de Rico.

The original grail scene designed by Paul von Jonkowsky and the Bruckner Brothers was used at Bayreuth from 1882 until 1933. While the Byzantine architecture roots the action in a particular historical moment, the dramatic shaft of light seems to lift the figure of Parsifal out of the physical world and into a divine space of his own.

Less can be more! In his Bayreuth Siegfried, Wieland Wagner's use of lighting to set the scene evoked an ancient Greek type of timelessness and universality. Within the abstract spaces, unmoored from any specifics of time and place, the Wagnerian drama unfolds like a dream for all of humanity.

Back-drop projections in Gunther Schneider-Siemssen's production of Das Rheingold and Die Walküre, for the Metropolitan Opera, allow the stage to be extended backwards into unending depths of stormy skies, flashing rainbows and climbing flames, so the audience cannot clearly tell where the physical stage ends and the fantastical imaginings begin. (Photos by Winnie Klotz).

Placido Domingo as Parsifal.

While the Metropolitan Opera's production of Parsifal retains the opulence of nineteenth century romantic naturalism, the luminescent grail is imbued with an other-worldly glow that symbolizes the light of spiritual wisdom, and removes the production from operatic realism. (Photo by Ken Howard).

63

BRUNHILDE'S IMMOLATION – ARTHUR RACKHAM

Many visual artists have been inspired by the very same aspects of Wagner's music-dramas that are the most challenging to depict on a solid stage. Here, in Arthur Rackham's depiction of Brünnhilde's immolation, the painter revels in the frenzied motion of the flames that envelop her, as she and her horse rise into an exalted, purifying blaze of glory.

DAS RHEINGOLD – U<small>L DE</small> R<small>ICO</small>

Ul de Rico employs a surreal framing device that compresses the narrative time into parallel scenes within the same frame, so two scenes comment on each other, highlighting ironies and similarities between them. The Rheinmaidens swirl around the eerily glowing Rheingold perched on an undersea pinnacle that mirrors the towers of Valhalla taking shape in the darkness above.

GÖTTERDÄMMERUNG – UL DE RICO

In "Götterdämmerung", as the walls of Valhalla crash down to earth, de Rico fills the canvas with a cacophony of destructive forces in a way that would be impossible on a physical sage. The tiny figure of Brünnhilde on her rearing horse is consumed by flames at the center of an explosion that unites heaven and earth in chaos.

GÖTTERDÄMMERUNG – Ul de Rico

Even fiercer, swirling motions fill the canvas in which de Rico depicts the triumph of the Rhein river over human greed. Enormous waves, glinting with firelight, dwarf the humans caught up in their swelling forces, and rise and fall with the grandeur of Wagner's thrilling orchestra.

67

TANNHÄUSER – Henri Fantin-Letour

Henri Fantin-Latour was normally a painter of precise naturalism, but not when he illustrated Wagner's music-dramas. His etching of "The Evening Star" applies a blurred, agitated texture, light-filled and impressionistic, to evoke a dreamlike state. The figure of Elizabeth appears to Wolfram as a phantom vision bathed in a divine light.

THE FLYING DUTCHMAN – HENRI FANTIN-LETOUR

Fantin-Latour's illustration depicting the final transcendence of Senta and the Dutchman is reminiscent of a Baroque angel escorting the resurrected man into heaven. While this image suggests a more traditional religious symbolism than Wagner would have welcomed, the way their individual forms begin to evaporate in the heavenly light does epitomize Wagnerian transcendence.

TRISTAN ANDE ISOLDE – HENRI FANTIN-LETOUR
In his depiction of Brangäne's anxious watch over Tristan and Isolde,
Fantin-Latour creates a deeply textured darkness that conceals the lovers and
nurtures their state of ecstasy in its mysterious hollows.

PARSIFAL – HENRI FANTIN-LETOUR
"Evocation of Kundry" shares a dreamlike quality with Fantin-Latour's other Wagner illustrations. In this etching, the sinuous form of Kundry emerges out of sleep into a hypnotized state, less as an individual than as an embodied spirit of longing and tortured sexuality.

CHAPTER EIGHT

THE WAGNER MOMENT:
A MYSTICAL EXPERIENCE

Now the question arises, given the mystical quality of much of Wagner's music, can the Wagnerian moments experienced by people susceptible to his music correctly be called "mystical experiences"? In the course of this book we have encountered all seven of the characteristics found by Professor Walter T. Stace in his *Mysticism and Philosophy* to be common to the mystical experiences of all cultures and times.

The Seven Characteristics of Mysticism:

1. The Unitary Conscious, the One the Void
   "personal identity dissolved in an infinite ocean of being".
2. Non-spatial – Non temperal.
3. Sense of objectivity or reality.
4. Blessedness or peace.
5. Feeling of being sacred or divine.
6. Parodoxicality.
7. Ineffable.

These same characteristics can be found if we examine the Wagner Moments already recorded starting with Charles Beaudelaire's quote at the beginning of this book. In addition to those of Chris Hunter, Claude DeBussy, and Jeffrey Swann quoted in chapter one, there are the following from J.K. Holman's book, *Wagner Moments:* which express the same characteristics:

Frederick A. Buechner: "I experienced the most wonderful calm, as if God were reaching his arms out from the stage to encircle, enfold, console and comfort the audience."(117)

Jonathon Lewsey: "This was like entering another world. Something...transported me...to the vast limitless horizons of Myth."[118]

Saul Lilienstein: "There has never been a more thrilling discovery of self and the greater world beyond the self...a world parallel to the real world in which all moment seems divinely ordered."[119]

Richard Mayer: "I was suddenly and profoundly overtaken. Clearly I was in awe of the entire experience, that moment. The tears could not express the depth of emotion I felt at that time. It was absolutely soulful and religious, as I felt in my heart I was experiencing total beauty. Perfection possibly. Maybe it was God speaking to me through the music. It was wonderful. It was the most perfect, most beautiful moment of my life. And I have that forever. Nothing will diminish that feeling nor take away the enrichment. What power to affect a person, a life, so profoundly."[120]

Alisdair Neale: "Time seemed to stand still, and the mystical quality of the score resonated within me in a way that I can't really articulate. But it was very real at the time – and the orchestra and I knew it without having said a word."[121]

Tim Page: "Time was suspended; and I was transformed...I thought, this is transcendental music."[122]

Thomas May: "Wagner resounded for me at once on levels that seemed physical, emotional and spiritual. The music's beauty and significance were palpably painful – precisely because they made sense, yet could not be explained. What seemed most obvious was that this was an art reaching to the core, with the capacity to change a life...This was music that made one look within...Individual discoveries hover in my memory with Proustian exactitud...and it is that paradoxical reconfirmation of sensual, finite boundaries and the time-defying replay that opens, as Chekhov might say, into infinity."[123]

A quote from Kenneth Hutton's lecture on Schopenhauer and Wagner delivered to the Wagner Society of Scotland in January of 2004 provides an appropriate summing up of all this:

We see through (Wagner's) art, a glimpse of this world as it is and are released from our blinkered human-centric viewpoint even if for a fleeting moment, where the world appears as one undifferentiated whole, where there is no distinction between the entity doing the thinking and the things being thought about, where philosophy, music, voice, stage performance and set meld into an indescribable Whole, greater than the sum of its parts, taking us out of and beyond ourselves, obliterating the distinction between subject and object and conveying something of the Ultimate to us.[124]

It appears from all that we have covered that these experiences are a kind of mystical experience...certainly not as extreme as those recorded by The Buddha, Plotinus, St. Francis or Jakob Boehme...possibly not as illuminating as those expressed by Robert Lewis Stevenson, Arthur Koestler or Alfred Lord Tennyson...but, nonetheless, a kind of mystical experience.

CHAPTER NINE

WAGNER'S INTENTIONS

Now the question – are these experiences something that Wagner intended or do they just happen? I was very fortunate in coming across a pamphlet by Jerry Sehulster, Professor of Psychology at the University of Connecticut. *The Role of Altered States of Consciousness in the Life, Theater and Theories of Richard Wagner.* Sehulster feels that what is being experienced is what psychologists call an "altered state of consciousness".

He points out that "Wagner's autobiography abounds with descriptions of trance, ecstasy, delirium, hypnagogic states, creative reveries, and wild dreams."(125)

Most of these are associated with music, and Wagner considers them to be mystical experiences. In describing his teen age years in his autobiography Wagner writes as follows:

In my sixteenth year, chiefly from a perusal of E.T.A. Hoffman's works, on fire with the maddest mysticism, I had visions by day in semi slumber, in which the keynote third and dominant seemed to be taking on living form and reveal to me their mighty meaning.(126)

The mysterious joy I felt in hearing an orchestra play quite close to me still remains one of my most pleasant memories. The tuning up of the instruments put me in a state of mystic excitement; even the striking of fifths on the violin seemed to me like a greeting from the spirit world – which, I may mention incidentally, had a very real meaning for me. When I was still almost a baby, the sound of these fifths, which had always excited me, was closely associated in my mind with ghosts and spirits.(127)

The hearing of Beethoven's Ninth's Symphony had a great impact in turning young Wagner's thoughts towards becoming a composer. He writes:

> Beethoven's Ninth Symphony became the mystical goal of all my strange thoughts and desires about music. I was first attracted to it by the opinion prevalent among musicians, not only in Leipzig but elsewhere, that this work had been written by Beethoven when he was already half mad. It was considered the *non plus ultra* of all that was fantastic and incomprehensible, and this was quite enough to rouse in me a passionate desire to study this mysterious work. At the very first glance at the score, of which I obtained possession with such difficulty, I felt irresistibly attracted by the long-sustained pure fifths with which the first phase opens: these chords, which, as I related above, had played such a supernatural part in my childish impressions of music, seemed in this case to form the spiritual keynote of my own life. This, I thought, must surely contain the secret of all secrets, and accordingly the first thing to be done was to make the score my own by a process of laborious copying.(128)

There is a question as to whether or not one of Wagner's best known altered states of consciousness actually happened. In his autobiography Wagner writes of an experience he had in La Spezia, Italy, in September of 1853 which gave him the inspiration for the famous E flat major chord beginning of the prelude to *Das Rheingold*:

> I sank into a kind of sonambulistic state, in which I suddenly had the feeling of being immersed in rapidly flowing water. Its rushing soon resolved itself for me into the musical sound of the chord of E flat major, resounding in persistent broken chords...I awoke in

sudden terror from this trance, feeling as though the
waves were crashing high above my head. I recognized
at once that the orchestral prelude to *Das Rheingold,* long
dormant within me but up to that moment inchoate,
had at last been revealed.(129)

Unfortunately, there is some question as to whether or not this
incredible experience ever happened because of an inconsistency in dates
and the fact that Wagner made no mention in his writings until fifteen
months after its supposed occurrence, including a letter to Liszt six
months later, saying simply that he had "adapted a totally different
approach...constructed on the simple triad of E flat."(130)

It has been conjectured that Wagner made up the story to impress
Emily Ritter, the daughter of Wagner's benefactress, Frau Julie Ritter.
The truth regarding this one incident probably will never be known,
but it is of little consequence in the total picture. There is plenty of
evidence that from childhood on, Wagner had experienced altered states
of consciousness.

Sehulster goes on to say that Wagner's dramas too, abound with
dramatizations of similar states of altered states of consciousness...
Senta's dreamy contemplation of the Dutchman's portrait and her state
of ecstasy when she realizes the Dutchman is seeking her. Tannhäuser
experiences trance, ecstasy, delirium and exhaustion during the course
of the drama. Elizabeth describes the emotions elicited by Tannhäuser's
(Wagner's), true art:

But what a strange new life your song conjured up
in my breast! Now it would thrill through me like pain,
now penetrate me like sudden joy. Emotions I had never
experienced! Longings I have never known! That which
once was dear vanished before a bliss nameless hereto-
fore! And when you left us then, peace and joy were
gone from me; the melodies the minstrels sang appeared
insipid to me, melancholy their temper. Dreaming, I

experienced heavy sorrow, my waking hours became a
troubled delusion, joy fled from my heart – Heinrich!
Heinrich! What had you done to me?[131]

In *Tristan*, not only do the two main characters experience altered
states of consciousness, but they discuss them at some length. They sing,
"I now then am the world." And, in a loss of identity, Tristan sings,
"I Isolde, you, Tristan."

Sehulster goes on to point out that Wagner "adopted Schopenhauer's
theory of creativity...that the artist perceives a world beyond
everyday waking reality. He attempts to communicate this world
to an audience by creating an art work. The art work is such that the
listener experiences a state similar to that of the artist when the work
was created...this being very intentional by the artist."[132]

Wagner developed the artistic means to accomplish this. In his 1870
essay, "Beethoven," Wagner writes about:

"the dream-like nature of the state into which we are
plunged through sympathetic hearing, and wherein that
dawns in us that other world, the world in which the
musician speaks to us. We recognize we have fallen into
a state essentially akin to that of hypnotic clairvoyance.
And, in truth, it is in this state alone that we immediately belong to the musician's world. From out of that
world, which nothing else can picture – the musician
casts the meshwork of his tone to net us, so to speak, or
with his wonder drops of sound, he dews our brain, as if
by magic, and robs us of the power of seeing ought to
save our own inner world."[133]

Sehulster points out the devices Wagner used to enhance the effect
of his "wonder drops of sound". Nietzsche referred to them as: "Wagner's
hypnotic tricks"...dimming the lights, doing away with the distraction
of applause, the disappearance of the orchestra, increasing the size of
the orchestra, making climaxes louder and more visible, raising the

temperature of a scene through sequencing and chromaticism; establishing a very regular and steady pace to his drama, an effect similar to the regular chanting of a prayer or the steady sounding of the surf... scenic changes without interpretation to the music...lengthening the dramas to distort the listener's sense of time. As Sehulster says, "a listener who has just spent four and one half hours in the dark, intensely concentrating on a powerful drama, is more likely to view the experience as spiritual, profound, or perhaps even mystical."(134)

Interestingly, even Wagner's critic, Eduard Hanslick, was impacted by Wagner's devices. In writing about his experience at Bayreuth, Hanslick wrote:

> "Wagner strives everywhere with the strongest sensual impression with every available means. The mysterious heaving of his invisible orchestra gives the listener a mild opium jag, even before the rising of the curtain. He is subjected to the enduring impression of a magically lighted fairy tale scene before anyone on the stage has opened his mouth. In the numerous night scenes, a dazzling light plays upon the figure of the principal characters, while tinted steam undulates upon and above the stage. This steam, which in *Das Rheingold*, even takes the place of the change of scene curtain, constitutes the most powerful weapon in Wagner's new dramatic arsenal. A formless, fantastic, sensually fascinating element, it has a special affinity with Wagner's musical principles. He, himself, compares the music emanating from his invisible orchestra with the 'steam' rising from Pythia's tripod, which introduces the listener to an exalted condition of clairvoyance. From here it is only a step to the artificial enjoyment of certain smells and odors. Psychology recognizes them as particularly stimulating and exciting."(135)

Sehulster concludes that Wagner clearly wanted to create in his listeners an altered state of consciousness.

Will Crutchfield in his 2003 *Opera News* article on Wagner and Bellini, wrote about some of Wagner's methods. Notice some of the words he chooses. "In Wagner, these wandering, unaccompanied lines roam farther and longer. They are descents into the subconscious. The long meditations in which we rest, digest, prepare ourselves for the next unfolding of the drama. I believe they are the likely key to the workability of Wagner's unprecedented long time span. Nobody could bear an opera six hours long if all of it had the intensity of Isolde's curse. But the long English horn solo while Tristan lies dying...the remote high-searching cry of the violins as Siegfried reaches the clearing at the top of the mountain...the cellos mournful meditation before the chorale tune in *Die Meistersinger*...the bass clarinet probing the depths of incomprehension as Brunnhilde mediates her plea to Wotan, or Marke his questioning reproach to Tristan...these are the pages that bring on an altered state. This kind of immersion, part ultra-methodical development, part trance-like rumination, has a lot to do with the authenticity we sense, the feeling that the music rings true."(136)

Undoubtedly, there were times when Wagner was composing that he was in an altered state of consciousness. Extreme altered states, such as described in the La Spezia incident, probably were rare if they existed at all. But Wagner's preoccupation with bringing the subconscious to the conscious...to grasp things intuitively before identifying them cognitively...tell us something about Wagner's compositional process.

In September, 1860, in *The Music of the Future*, Wagner writes about the "the presenting forces being unconscious...intrinsic"...

> If we may regard all nature, looked as a whole, as a
> process of development from the unconscious to con-
> sciousness, and if this process appears most conspicuously
> in the human individual, the observation of it in the life
> of the artist is certainly one of the most interesting,

because in him and his creations the world represents itself and comes to conscious existence. But in the artist, too, the presenting force is in its very nature unconscious – instinctive; and even where he requires thought in order to form the outline of his intuition, by the aid of the technical ability with which he is endowed, into an objective work of art, it is not exactly reflection that decides for him the choice of his means of expression, but rather an instinctive impulse, which constitutes, indeed, the character of his peculiar talent.(137)

Thematic ideas and motifs would come to him spontaneously and at odd moments, and he would write them down quickly on whatever scrap of paper might be handy at that moment, unlike Beethoven, for example, where musical ideas were carefully noted in his sketch book. With the exception of *Tristan*, Wagner, in all of his mature works, wrote a prose scenario and the libretto before composing the music, but the music was already swimming in his head before he did this.

The biographer Curt Von Westernhagen wrote that Wagner in his creative process would suddenly see the work in its totality with text, music and staging all occurring at the same time "like an improvised performance in his imagination." The poet, John Masefield, has described a similar genesis in his creative process as a sudden ineffable illumination:

Instantly the poem appeared to me in its complete form, with every detail distinct...this illumination is an intense experience so wonderful that it cannot be described, while it lasts the momentary problem is merged into a dazzling clear perception of the entire work in all its detail. In a moment of ecstasy the writer...perceives what seems to be an unchangeable way of statement...it is a perception by a mortal of an undying reality...from which beauty, good,

wisdom, and rightness come to man...certainly to
myself this last is the explanation...that this universe
of glory and energy exists and that man may in some
strange way enter into it and partake of its nature.(138)

As is the case with most mystical experiences Masefield finds the
experience ineffable but has the urge to describe it in an attempt to share
the experience with others.

As early as 1844 while beginning to work on *Tannhäuser* Wagner
wrote to his friend Karl Gaillard:

Even before I set about writing a single line of the
text or drafting a scene, I am already thoroughly im-
mersed in the musical aura of my new creation. I have
the whole sound and all the characteristic motives in my
head so that when the poem is finished and the scenes
are arranged in their proper order the actual opera is
already completed and its detailed execution of the
work is more a question of *calm and reflective revision*, the
moment of actual creativity having already passed.(139)

The "calm and reflective revision" was not as easy as Wagner
would like us to think. Ferdinand Praeger, writes in his book,
Wagner as I Knew Him:

He did not shake the notes from his pen as pepper
from a caster. How could it otherwise than labour with
a man holding such views as his? Listen to what he says
'For a work to live, to go down to future generations,
it must be reflective...a composer, in planning and
working out a great idea, must pass through a kind
of parturition (child birth)'...he went to the piano
with his idea already in mind, and made the piano
his sketchbook wherein he worked and reworked his
subject, steadily modeling his matter until it assumed
the shape he had in mind.(140)

Thomas Mann in his *Suffering and Greatness of Richard Wagner* quotes Wagner further on the subject of "reflection":

> We should not underestimate the power of reflection; the unconsciously produced work of art belongs to a period remote from ours and the art product of the most highly cultivated period cannot be produced otherwise than in full consciousness."(141)

Wagner's compositional method was a combination of a "presenting force in its very nature unconscious – instinctive", and reflective hard work shaping the results.

As Thomas Mann concludes:

> In short, his author- and creator-ship has contact with both spheres, the one that lies 'remote from ours'. As well as the one where the brain long ago developed into the modern intellectual tool we know. And hence the indissoluble mingling of the dæmonic and the bourgeois is the essence of him.(142)

Bryan Magee describes Wagner's creative process as follows:

> "He placed complete trust in his unconscious as an artist, believing that if he gave himself up completely to its powerful workings everything would come right in the end…The crucial point is that the artistic material, the *"Stoff "*, was spontaneously created: it came to him, and he let it come. His conscious mind played little or no part in its creation. What his mind did was work on that material with all the intelligence and craftsmanship at its command, structuring, organizing, interrelating, integrating, transposing, shaping, polishing."(143)

In his intermission commentary during a Metropolitan Opera broadcast, Father Owen Lee summed up *Die Meistersinger* as follows:

> Art for Richard Wagner is fashioned from both intuition and honest craftsmanship, from both innova-

tive spirit and respect for tradition. It can speak power-
fully to us if we have within ourselves the capacity to
respond to it. It can survive the fall of empires to speak
to future generations about the civilization that produced it. It can tell us what we need to know about ourselves, perhaps most of all about the flaw in human
nature that makes mysteries of our lives. And it can help
us to accept the inevitable sadness in life – as well as to
sing like songbirds from the sheer joy of being alive.(144)

For years Father Lee, a Catholic priest, has entertained and educated
opera audiences and readers through his commentaries and published
works. Many of them deal with mystical and spiritual aspects of
Wagner's music dramas.

Wagner's musical compositions were for himself a kind of mystical
experience. What he felt subconsciously and intuitively would be expressed musically in terms that often he himself could not explain cognitively. And he *did* want this mystical experience to be shared with others.
As early as 1840 at the age of twenty-seven while in Paris he wrote:

How explain the demonic compulsion which drives
the genius to hawk his most treasured possessions? No
doubt the paramount factor, the one which alone sustains
him in the darkest hours, is a Godlike impulse to communicate his own inner bliss to the hearts of all men.(145)

The next year while still in Paris he wrote in his own version of the
Apostolic Creed:

"I believe in the Holy Spirit and God, and the one
indivisible art...I believe that he who once has bathed
in the sublime delights of this high act, is consecrated
to Her forever, and never can deny Her."(146)

These words are written with the passion of a young man who
already has discovered a mission in life to which he will be consecrated...a man who would maintain that passion and belief in himself

and his mission in the years to come through disappointment and despair – to the very end.

In 1853, reflecting upon the new course he had taken with *The Flying Dutchman*, a complete departure from his previous operas including the well-received *Rienzi*, Wagner wrote: "My course was new but was bidden by my inner mood and forced upon me by the pressing need to impart the mood to others," and impart the mood he did.[147]

In 1870 in his essay, *Beethoven*, Wagner writes

> The musician is controlled, as it were, by an urgent impulse to impart the vision of his inmost dreams... Only from an awkward side of consciousness can the intellect derive its ability to seize the Character of things...We are conscious of the existence of a second world, perceptible only through the ear, manifesting itself through sound...It is this inner life through which we are directly allied with the whole of Nature and these are brought into a relation with the Essence of things that eludes the forms of outer knowledge, time and space...[148]

> Music draws us at once from any concern with the relation of things outside us and – as pure form set free from Matter – shuts us off from the outside world as it were, to let us gaze into the inmost Essence of ourselves and of all things..."[149]

> We here are given an image almost as timeless as it is spaceless an altogether spiritual revelation; and the reason why it moves us so indivisibly is that, more plainly than all other things, it brings to our consciousness the inmost essence of Religion free from all dogmatic fictions."[150]

These passages from Wagner's *Beethoven* contain several of the seven basic characteristics of all mystic experiences as outlined by Walter T. Stace in his *Philosophy and Mysticism*.

Clearly, Wagner Moments are a type of mystical experience shared by many music lovers and Wagner himself intended this to happen.

CHAPTER TEN

THE SECOND PUZZLE

What about our *second puzzle* – the quote from Wagner's letter to Nietzsche. What is the great *renaissance*? Why combine Homer and Plato to bring this about?

From the time of his early school days' translation of *The Odyssey* Wagner was an admirer of Homer and the Greek tragedians. There are many parallels between Homer's *Odyssey* and *Iliad* in Wagner's music dramas. To name a few:

Like Odysseus, the Flying Dutchman, wanders in the search for home. Similarly, Parsifal searches for Montsalvat.

Venus keeps Tannhäuser in her grotto; eventually he returns to Elizabeth. Calypso keeps Odysseus on her island. Eventually he returns to Penelope.

The doctrine of guest friendship found in both the *Iliad* and *Odyssey* is present in the Wanderer scene in *Siegfried* and the first act of *Die Walküre.*

The Homeric Gods are Gods of a mountain just as the Gods of *The Ring* are associated with rocky cliffs. They are storm Gods, and Zeus employs lighting and thunder to demonstrate his power just as Wotan does in the Wanderer scene and the second act of Die Walküre.

Hera's belittling of Zeus in the *Iliad* is remarkably similar to the Fricka-Wotan dialogue in the second act of *Die Walküre.*

The Homeric Gods interfere with battle and protect their heroes in a fashion similar to Wotan's and Brunhilde's actions in *Die Walküre.*

The Gods are not free but are responsible to fate. Thus Zeus holds up the scales of fate, and Wotan seeks the advice of Erda.

Achilles, like Siegfried, is the supreme hero with a God and a human as parents. They each have only one weak spot where they can be killed...Achilles' heel and Siegfried's back.

Achilles' struggle with Hector is doomed to result in destruction just as Wotan's struggle to regain the ring is destined to lead to the twilight of the Gods.

Achilles must pay for his sin of selfishness – satisfying his personal whims before attending to the welfare of his people. Wotan's lust for power leads to his downfall.

The Cyclops curses Odysseus in a manner similar to Alberich's curse of Wotan.

The pity of Hector's death is that Zeus cannot prevent it just as Wotan is bound by oath and must bring about the death of Siegmund.

The closing scene of the *Iliad* and finds Achilles and Priam both bereft and destroyed, faced with the stark reality of the tragedy of mankind – a situation comparable to that at the end of *Götterdämmerung*.

In 1848, Wagner had renewed his study of the Greek language. In re-reading the *Iliad* and the *Odyssey* in the original Greek, he had to have noticed that Homer used a leit motif type system in which people and places had phrases associated with them which were repeated throughout the works…phrases such as Menelaus *the warlike*, Troy *where the soil is rich, horse-pasturing Argos*, and Achia, *the land of fair women*. Homer's works were conceived to be recited aloud, and these phrases also were designed to fit the metre of the poetry. They are, therefore, both informational and pleasant to the ear as well…not unlike Wagner's leit motifs.

Wagner seriously considered a work based on Achilles. In his auto-biography he writes that during the 1849 Dresden uprising he was thinking of "material for dramas, *Achilleus*, which has occupied me for some time." Nothing ever came from this as Wagner turned to *The Ring* instead, but sixteen years later, in 1865, he mentioned it in a letter to King Ludwig.

Wagner undoubtedly felt that he was creating music dramas which were epics in the Homeric tradition – epics which dealt with the universal, the eternal, the timeless and, which "would be there for all time with a stamp of eternity on every episode."

Plato, of course, also had a great influence on Wagner, but the thought of Plato embracing Homer at first seems rather strange. After all, Plato spent a great deal of time in *The Republic* criticizing Homer. And whereas Plato's dialogues dealt mostly with things from the head – wisdom and reasoning – Homer's epics dealt mostly with the things from the heart – feelings, if you will.

But remember that what interested Wagner was Plato's metaphysics...that there is another world beyond the world of our senses – the real world of Ideas which is outside of time and space..and Plato's mystical thoughts expressed in *The Symposium* that this world could be discovered by the individual within himself. Thus, Plato will embrace Homer,...the use of the epic to express feeling,...but Homer in turn will be imbued with the mystical platonic spirit of *The Symposium,* enabling us to discover Plato's eternal ideas within ourselves.

Could the result of all this, the great renaissance or rebirth, be the Wagner Moment?

I wrote to Bryan Magee concerning this. He wrote back to me as follows: "Wagner thought he was bringing philosophy and art together at the highest level, the level of Plato (representing philosophy) and Homer (representing art)."

I am comfortable with that response and also feel that it is fully compatible with the idea that the great renaissance is accomplished in combining the best of Homer and Plato to bring about a Wagner moment.

EPILOGUE

WAGNER'S GRAIL: HIS GREAT ART

"No master wrote this.
It was a god who gave this music birth...
This joy must be felt by all the world.
No greater dream was ever dreamed.
Then would the people on this earth
Be remade and redeemed."

– Rudolph Sabor, *(Wagner Moments)*

It took Wagner half his life to get *Parsifal* on the stage, from the time he first conceived of it at Marienbad in 1845 to its completion and first performance in 1882. He knew and stated that it would be his last stage work. Cosima referred to it as "the crowning achievement".

It was a culmination and distillation of all the mystical thoughts he had encountered or developed over the years. These were the results of his continued intellectual curiosity, his study of religions, and his extensive readings, particularly those of Plato, Feuerbach, Hafiz, Schopenhauer, Eckhart and the eastern mystics – plus his constant striving to sort out his thinking and to try to put it into words, even though he often felt it to be ineffable.

He had found that through his music all the threads of the Wagner fabric could knit together and his mystic message be conveyed to his audiences so that they could have the same "spiritual revelation" that Wagner the Mystic had had, and share with him his "inner mood" the "vision of his inmost dreams" and the "inmost Essence of ourselves and of all things."

Wagner himself is portrayed in many of his operas – the misunderstood artist, an outsider to conventional society, often seeking redemption (deliverance) through the unequivocal love of a woman. I believe that in the culmination of his life's work, Wagner, the mystic, saw himself as Parsifal. Wagner's Grail is his great art, which he holds up to us for us to experience, with the hope that we, too, can be redeemed from the everyday, nitty-gritty, phenomenal world...become knowers through feeling, and in an altered state of consciousness, discover within ourselves, that which is universal, eternal, and timeless. That is an incredible task for a composer to undertake. What is even more incredible, is that those of us who are susceptible to his art know, when we have this feeling of wholeness, yet unboundedness, ineffable but real...that he was successful.

Index

A

Aberback, Alan David 12, 22-23
Achilles 89-90
Aeschylus 12, 14
Aesthetics 37, 39
Anagogy 21
Anders, Alloy 44

B

Bach, *St. Matthew Passion* 43
Bailey, Robert 55
Beaudelaire, Charles 1, 3, 73
Beethoven 28, 78
Bellini, Vincenzo 82
Bernouf, Ernest 47, 50
Boehm, Jacob 48, 75
Buddhism 31, 34-35, 47, 49,
      50-52, 75
Buechner, Frederick A. 73
Bulow, Hans Von 45
Byron 21, 36

C

Campbell, Joseph 23
Cavendish, Richard 23
Carrolsfeld, Ludwig
      Schnorr von and
      Malvina 44
Cervantes 11, 12, 14
Chausson, Ernest 45

Cooke, Deryck 35, 36
Crutchfield, Will 82

D

DeBussy, Claude 2, 73
Dramaturgy 21
Dionysic religion 17-18

E

Eckhart, Meister 12, 47-48, 93
Ellis, W. Ashton 11, 15
Engels, Frederick 29
Epistemology 2
Erlœsung 22, 27, 51
Eschenbach, Wolfrom von
      23, 53

F

Feeling 28-29, 37, 94
Feuerbach, Ludwig von 25-29,
      33, 37, 93
Fichte, Johann Gottlieb 14
Flying Dutchman 22, 26, 27, 69,
      79, 87, 89
Franck, Cesar 45

G

Gaillard, Karl 84
Glasenapp 11
Gnostics 17-18, 27, 48

Gobineau, Count de 50
Goethe 11, 14, 36, 49
Goldman, Albert 21-22
Gorres, Joseph Von 22
Götterdämmerung 34-37, 57, 59,
   66, 67, 90
Grail 23-24, 93-94

H
Hafiz 30-31, 55, 93
Hanslick, Eduard 81
Hegel, Friedrich 28
Herwegh, George 33
Hinduism 7, 47-50
Hoffman, E.T.A. 77
Holman, J.K. III 2, 73
Homer 6, 13, 14, 15, 16, 18-19,
26, 89-91
Hunter, Chris 2, 73
Hutton, Kenneth 74-75

I
Illiad 15, 89-90
Illuminati 48-49

J
James, William 7
Jesus of Nazareth 27-28, 43, 47,
   48, 53

K
Kandinsky, Wassily 24-25
Kant, Emmanuel 37-38
Koestler, Arthur 75

L
La Spezia 78-79, 82
Lee, Father Owen 4, 6, 85-86
Lewsey, Jonathon 74
Lilienstein, Saul III, 54, 74
Liszt, Franz 24, 41, 45, 49
Lohengrin 22, 23-24, 27, 54
Ludwig, King 26, 52

M
Magee, Bryan III, 3, 5, 22,
   40, 85
Maier, Matilda 53
Mann, Thomas 33, 85
Marienbad 23, 53, 93
Marx, Karl 29
Masefield, John 83-84
Matthews, John 23
Mayer, Richard 74
May, Thomas 74
Meistersinger, Die 2-3, 14, 37-38,
   85-86
Metaphysics 2-3, 14, 16, 21, 39
Metropolitan Opera 45, 62-63
Meyerbeer 11
Mitleid 52
Mozart 59

Mysticism 7, 14, 21, 28, 48
  Definition 3, 29
  Seven Characteristics 7-9,
    14, 73
Myth 15-16

N
Neale, Alisdair 74
Neo Platonism 7
Newman, Ernest 6, 11, 33, 43
Nietzsche, Friedrich 4-6, 33,
  80, 89
Novalis 22, 41

O
Oats, J. Whitney III
Odyssey 13, 15, 89-90
One, The 8, 48, 73
Ontology 2

P
Page, Tim 74
Paradox 3, 9, 73
Parsifal 22, 26-27, 37, 52-55,
  60, 61, 63, 71, 89, 93-94
Plato 6, 14, 15-16, 37, 89,
  91, 93
    Republic 16-19
    Symposium 14, 19-21, 27,
      51, 91
Plotinus 75
Porges, Heinrich 51

Porter, Andrew 34
Praeger, Ferdinand 84
Pythagoras 17, 18, 27

Q
Quantum Physics 55

R
Rackham, Arthur 64
Redemption 22, 27, 51-53
Religion 25-26, 30
Rheingold, Das 62, 78-79, 81
Rico, Ul de 65-67
Rienzi 87
Ring 22, 29, 34, 38, 89
Ritter, Emily and Julia 79
Röeckel, August 30, 34, 35,
  52-53
Rosicrucians 49

S
Sabor, Rudolph 93
Sachs, Hans 48
Saint Francis 75
Schofield, Paul 50
Schelling, Friedrich 22
Schilling, August 28
Schlegel brothers 22
Schneider-Siemssen,
  Gunther 59-62
Schopenhauer, Arthur 15,
  33-40, 42, 47, 93

Schubert, G.H. von 22
Sehulster, Jerome III, 77-81
Shakespeare 14
Sieger, Die 50-51
Siegfried 51, 61, 89
Smith, Huston 7-8
Sophocles 14
Stace, Walter T. III, 7-9, 42,
  73, 87
Stevenson, Robert Lewis 75
Sufism 7
Swann, Jeffrey 2, 41-43, 73

T
Tanhäuser VII, 1, 22, 27, 68,
  79-80, 84, 89
Tanner, Michael 2-4, 23-24,
  41-43
Tauler, Johannes 48-49
Taylor, A.E. 19, 21
Time and Space 8, 54-55, 73, 87
Tristan and Isolde 37, 38, 41-45,
  54, 70, 80, 83

U
Uhlig, Theodore 31
Unconscious to conscious
  28-29, 39
Upanishads, The 47-48, 49, 50

W
Wagner, Cosima 12, 16, 20 45,
  48, 55, 59, 93
Wagner Moments 2, 5, 24,
  73-75, 88
Wagner, Richard
  Difficulties in Writing
    12-13
  Dresden Library 11

  Prose works:
  Art and Revolution 30
  Art Work of the Future 29
  Beethoven 80, 87
  Music of the Future 82-83
  On State and Religion 49
  Opera and Drama 15, 54-55
  Religion and Art 18, 26
  The Public in Time and Space 59
Wagner, Siegfried 48
Wagner, Wieland 61
Wagner Societies 5
Walkure, Die 36, 62, 89
Weissheimer, Wendelin 53
Welsh, Roy Dickinson III, 5
Wessendonk, Matilda 20, 49,
  51-52, 53, 83
Westernhagen, Count von 83
Whitehead, A.N. 17

X
Xenophanes 26

BIBLIOGRAPHY

Aberback, Allan David. 2003 [1988]. *The Ideas of Richard Wagner.* University Press of America.

Armstrong, Karen. 1993. *A History of God: The 4000-Year Quest of Judaism Christianity and Islam.* New York: Ballantine Books.

Barth, / Moch, / Voss, Herbert. / Dietrich. / Egon. 1975. *Wagner, A Documentary.* Oxford University Press.

Beckett, Lucy. 1981. *Richard Wagner: Parsifal.* Cambridge: Cambridge University Press.

Bekker, Paul. 1931 [1924]. *Richard Wagner: His Life in His Work.* Trans. M.M. Bozman. New YorK: W.W. Norton and Co.

Bell, Gertrude Lowthian. 2007 [1897]. *The Teachings of Hafiz.* BiblioBazaar.

Borchmeyer, Dieter. 2002 [1991]. *Richard Wagner, Theory and Theater.* Trans. Stewart Spencer. Oxford University Press.

Burbidge, / Sutton, Peter. / Richard. 1979. *The Wagner Companion. (Edited by Peter Bruhidge and Richard Sutton).* Cambridge University Press.

Burlingame, Edward L. 1875. *Art Life and Theories of Richard Wagner.* New York: Henry Holt and Company.

Butler, Jeffery. 2001. *Classically Romantic, Classical Form and Meaning In Wagner's Ring.* Philadelphia: Xlibris Corporation.

Campbell, Joseph. 1968. *The Masks of God: Creative Mythology.* Penguin Books.

Capra, Fritjof. 2000 [1975]. *The Tao of Physics: An Exploration of the Parallels Between Modern Physics and Eastern Mysticism.* Boston: Shambhala.

Carnegy, Patrick. 2006. *Wagner and the Art of the Theater.* Yale University Press.

Chamberlain, Houston Stuart. 1900. *Richard Wagner.* London: J.M. Dent and Co.

Cooke, Deryck. 1979. *I Saw the World End.* New York: Oxford University Press.

Cord, William O. 1998 [1983]. *An Introduction to Richard Wagner's Der Ring des Nibelergen (second edition).* Athens: Ohio University Press.

Crutchfield, Will. 2003 (Feb.) *Unbroken Line.* Opera News.

Dalhaus, Carl. 1971. *Richard Wagner's Music Dramas.* Cambridge University Press.

Deathridger / Dalhaus, John. / Carl. 1984. *The New Groove Wagner.* NewYork: W. Norton & Company.

Di Gaetani, John L. 1978. *Penetrating Wagner's Ring (Edited by Di Gaetani.* New York: Da Capo Press, Inc.

Donnington, Robert. 1963. *Wagner's 'Ring' and it's Symbols.* New York: St. Martin's Press.

Eckermann, John Peter. 1930. *Conversations of Goethe with Eckermann.* Trans. John Oxenford. London:

Eckhart, Meister. 1996. *Meister Eckhart from Whom God Hid Nothing (Edited by David O'Neal).* Shambhala.

Eckhart, Meister. 1981. *The Essential Sermons, Commenataries,Treatises, and Defense.* Trans. Edmund Colledge and Bernard McGinn. Paulist Press.

Evans, Michael. 1982. *Wagner and Aeschylus, The Ring and the Orestia.* Cambridge University Press.

Everett, Derrick. 2001. *Parsifal: Under the Bodhi Tree.* United Kingdom: The Wagner Society of the United Kingdom (July issue).

Feurnbach, Ludwig. 1986. *Principles of the Philosophy of the Future.* Trans. Manfred H. Vogel. Hacket Publishing Co., Inc.

Freke, / Gandy, Timothy. / Peter. 1999. *The Jesus Mysteries: Was the "Orignal Jesus" a Pagan God?.* New York: Three Rivers Press.

Fricke, Richard. 1998. *Wagner in Rehearsal 1875-1876.* Pendragon Press.

Gardiner, Patrick. 1971 [1967]. *Schopenhauer.* Penguin Books Ltd.

Garten, H.F. 1977. *Wagner the Dramatist.* London: John Calder.

Gautier, Judith. 1910. *Wagner at Home.* London: Mills and Boon Ltd.

Gilbert, R.A. 1992. *The Elements of Mysticism.* Great Britain: Element Books Inc.

Glasenapp, C.F. 1902. *Life of Richard Wagner.* Trans. William Ashton Ellis. London: Kegan Paul, Trench, Truener and Co., Inc.

Goldman, / Sprinchorn, Albert. / Evert. 1964. *Wagner on Music and Drama.* New York: Da Capo Press, Inc.

Griffin, Jasper. 1980. *Homer.* Oxford University Press.

Hafiz. 2004. *Hafiz: The Mystic Poets.* Trans. Gertrude Bell. Vermont: SkyLight Paths Publishing.

Holman, J.K. 2007. *Wagner Moments: A Celbration of Favorite Wagner Experiences.* New York: Amadeus Press.

Holman, J.K. 1996. *Wagner's Ring: A Listener's Compsnion and Concordance.* Portland: Amadeus Press.

Hutton, Kenneth. 2006. *Schopenhauer.* United Kindom: The Wagner Society of the United Kingdom (August issue), page 10.

Janaway, Christopher. 1994. *Schopenhauer.* Oxford University Press.

Jullien, Adolph. 1892. *Richard Wagner: His Life Art and Works.* Boston: J.B. Millet Co.

Kahn, Charles H. 2001. *Pythagoras and the Pythagoreans.* Indianapolis: Hacket Publishing Co., Inc.

Kitcher, / Schocht, Philip. / Richard. 2004. *Finding An Ending.* Oxford University Press.

Kohler, Joachim. 1998. *Nietzsche and Wagner.* Yale University Press.

Kropsfinger, Klaus 1991. *Wagner and Beethoven.* Trans. Peter Palmer. Cambridge University Press.

Lattimore, Richmond. 1973 [1951]. *The Iliad of Homer.* Trans. Richmond Lattimore. Chicago: The University of Chicago Press.

Lee, M. Owen. 2007. *Wagner and the Wonder of Art: An Introduction to Die Meistersinger.* Toronto: University of Toronto Press.

Lee, M. Owen. 1999. *Wagner: The Terrible Man and His Terrible Art.* University of Toronto Press Inc.

Lee, M. Owen. 2003. *Athena Sings, Wagner and the Greeks.* University of Toronto Press Inc.

Lee, M. Owen. 1990. *Wagner's Ring: Turning the Sky Around.* Summit Books.

Lilienstein, Saul. *Parsifal: Commentary on C.D.* Washington National Opera.

Magee, Bryan. 1997 [1983]. *The Philosophy of Schopenhauer.* New York: Oxford University Press.

Magee, Bryan. 2000. *The Tristan Chord: Wagner and Philosophy.* New York: Metropolitan Books.

Magee, Bryan. 1999 [1992]. *Confessions of a Philosopher.* Modern Library.

Magee, Bryan. 1988 [1963]. *Aspects of Wagner.* Oxford University Press.

Mann, Thomas. 1957 [1929]. *Essays by Thomas Mann.* Trans. H.T. Lowe-Porter. New York: Vintage Books.

Matthews, John. 1990. *The Elements of the Grail Tradition.* Element Books Ltd.

Matthews, John (Editor). 1990. *The Household of the Grail Tradition.* Aquarian Press.

May, Thomas. 2004. *Decoding Wagner.* New Jersey: Amadeus Press.

Miller, / Ulrich, / Wopnewski, 1992. *Wagner Handbook (Edited by Miller, Ulrich, and Wopnewski).* Harvard University Press.

Millington, Barry. 1992. *The Wagner Compositions (Edited by Millington).* New York: Schirmer Books.

Newman, Ernest. 1931. *Fact and Fiction About Wagner.* New York: Alfred A. Knopf.

Newman, Ernest. 1930. *Stories of the Great Operas.* New York: Garden City Publishing Co.

Newman, Ernest. 1942 [1933]. *The Life of Richard Wagner.* New York: Alfred A. Knopf.

Newman, Ernest. 1924. *Wagner as Man and Artist.* Prosceniam Publishers Inc.

Nietzsche, Friedrich. 1956. *The Birth of Tragedy.* Trans. Francis Gulffing. Random House.

Nietzsche, Friedrich. 1982 {1954}. *The Portable Nietzsche.* Edited and Trans. Walter Kaufman. Penguin Books Ltd.

Nietzsche, Friedrich. 1921. *The Nietzsche-Wagner Correspondence. (Edited by Elizabeth Foerster-Nietzsche).* Trans. Caroline V. Kerr. Boni and Liveright.

Porges, Heinrich. 1983 [1876]. *Wagner Rehearsing the 'Ring': An Eye-Witness Account of the Stage Rehearsals of the First Beyreuth Festival.* Trans. Robert L. Jacobs. Cambridge: Cambridge University Press.

Pourtales, Guy de. 1932. *Richard Wagner.* Harper Bros. Publisher.

Praeger, Ferdinand. 1892. *Wagner As I Knew Him.* New York: Longmans, Green and Co.

Rather, L.J. 1972. *The Dream of Self-Destruction - Wagner's Ring and the Modern World.* Louisiana State University Press.

Rico, Ul de. 1980. *The Ring of the Nieblung: Wagner's Epic Drama.* New York: Thames and Hudson, Inc.

Sabor, Rudolph. 1989 [1987]. *The Real Wagner.* Cardinal: Sphere Books.

Schacht, Richard. 1995. *Making Sense of Nietzsche.* University of Illinois Press.

Schofield, Paul. 2007. *The Redeemer Reborn.* Amadeus Press.

Schopenhauer, Arthur. 2001 [1995]. *The World as Will And Idea.* Trans. Jill Berman. London: J.M. Dent.

Scruton, Roger. 2001 [1982]. *Kant.* Oxford University Press.

Sehulster, Jerome. 1980. *The Role of Altered States of Consciousness in the Life, Theatre, and Theories of Richard Wagner.* Baywood Publishing Co., Inc.

Sehulster, Jerome. 2001. *Richard Wagner's Creative Vision at LaSpezia.* Amsterdam/Philadelphia: John Benjamins Publishing Company.

Smith, Patrick J. 1975 [1970]. *The Tenth Muse: A Historical Study of the Opera Libretto.* New York: Schirmer Books.

Spencer, Stewart. 2000. *Wagner Remembered.* London: Faber and Faber.

Stace, Walter T. 1960. *The Teachings of the Mystics.* New York. New American Library Mentor.

Stace, W.T. 1960. *Mysticism and Philosophy.* Los Angeles: Jeremy P. Tarcher, Inc.

Stern, Jack. 1960. *Richard Wagner and the Synthesis of the Arts.* Wayne State University Press.

Swann, Jeffrey. *Tristan and the Mystic Experience (C.D. lecture)* New York: Wagner Society of New York.

Tanner, Michael. 1994. *Nietzsche.* Oxford University Press.

Tanner, Michael. 2009. *Then I Myself am the World: Wagner's Opera Metaphysicism* Glyndebourne: Glyndebourne Festival program, 2009, page 116.

Tanner, Michael. 1996. *Wagner.* Princeton: Princeton University Press.

Taylor, A.E. 1958 [1956]. *Plato: The Man and His Work.* New York: Meridian Press.

Taylor, Ronald. 1983. *Richard Wagner: His Life Art and Thought.* Panther Books.

Treadwell, James. 2003. *Interpreting Wagner.* Yale University Press.

Von Westernhagen, Curt. 1976 [1973]. *The Forging of the Ring.* Trans. Arnold and Mary Whittall. London: Cambridge University Press.

Wagner, Richard. 1896. *Prose Works. (Vols. I - VIII).* Trans. William Ashton Ellis. Kegan Paul, Trench, Truener and Co., Inc.

Wagner, Cosima. 1980. *Diaries. (Vols. I and II).* Harcourt Bruce Jovanovich, Inc.

Wagner, Richard. 1973. *Wagner Writes from Paris.* Edited and Trans. Robert L. Jacobs and Geoffrey Skelton. London: George Allen and Unwin Ltd.

Wagner, Richard. 1980. *The Brown Book - The Diary of Richard Wagner 1865-1882. (Presented and Annotated by Joachin Beyfield).* Trans. George Bird. Cambridge University Press.

Wagner, Richard. 1911. *My Life.* New York: Dodd Mead and Co.

Wagner, Richard. 1909. *Letters to Minna Wagner.* Trans. William Ashton Ellis. Charles Scribners and Sons.

Wagner, Richard. 1888. *Wagner - Liszt Correspondences (Vols. I & II)* Trans. Francis Hueffer. London: H. Grevel and Co.

Wagner, Richard. 1890. *Letters to Uhlig, Fisher and Heine.* Trans. J.S. Shedlock. London: H. Grevel and Co.

Wagner, Richard. *Richard Wagner's Letters to August Roeckel.* Trans. Eleanor C. Sellar. Bristol: J.W. Arrowsmith.

Wagner, Richard. 1988 [1987]. *Selected Letters of Richard Wagner.* Trans. Stewart Spencer and Barry Millington. New York: W.W. Norton & Company.

Wilson, Pearl Cleveland. 1919. *Wagner's Drama's and Greek Tragedy.* New York: Columbia University Press.

Winkler, Franz E. 1974. *For Freedom Destined: Mysteries of Man's Evolution in the Mythology of Wagner's Ring Operas and Parsifal.* New York: The Myrin Institute.

Zuckerman, Elliott. 1964 [1962]. *The First Hundred Years of Wagner's Tristan.* New York: Columbia University Press.

Upanishads, The. 1959 [1948] Trans. Swami Prabhavananda and Frederick Manchester. The Vendetta Society of Southern California.

NOTES

CD   Cosima's Diaries
CL   Collected Letters of Richard Wagner
MP   Mysticism and Philosophy
RAS   Role of Altered States
RW   Richard Wagner's Prose Works
TC   Tristan Chord
WM   Wagner Moments

1. *Richard Wagner,* edited by Herbert Barth, Dietrich Moch, and Egon Voss, page 193.
2. W.M., page 94.
3. Ibid, page 49.
4. Ibid, pages 92-93.
5. *Aspects of Wagner,* Bryan Magee, page 39.
6. Ibid, page 40.
7. *Wagner*, Michael Tanner, page 5.
8. *Wagner: The Terrible Man and His Truthful Art,* M. Owen Lee, pages 23-24.
9. *Nietzsche Contra Wagner,* Friedrich Nietzsche, page 667.
10. *The Real Wagner,* Rudolph Sabor, page 351.
11. *The Nietzsche-Wagner Correspondence,* page 39.
    (Philology is a word which is not much used today.
    It is basically classical studies, and Nietzche, in 1870,
    was one of the leading classical scholars in Germany).
12. M.P., pages 42-43.
13. Ibid, pages 5-6.
14. Ibid, page 7.
15. Ibid, pages 57 and 83.

16. Ibid, page 99.
17. Ibid, page 67 and 145.
18. Ibid, page 171.
19. Ibid, page 105.
20. *Parsifal, Lohengrin and the Legend of the Holy Grail,* Alice Leighton Cleather and Basil Crump, pages 181-182.
21. *The Real Wagner,* Rudolph Sabor, page 243.
22. *The Ideas of Richard Wagner,* Alan David Aberback, page 409.
23. *Wagner and Beethoven,* Klaus Kropfinger, page 70.
24. TC, page 67.
25. RW VIII, *Pasticcio,* page 65.
26. *Wagner Writes from Paris—A Happy Ending,* page 187.
27. RW II, page 191, *Opera and Drama.*
28. CD II, page 476.
29. *Pythagoras and the Pythagoreans,* Charles H. Rahn, page 1.
30. RW VI, page 231.
31. *The Republic* II, 378 b-e
32. Ibid III, 391c-392a
33. Ibid X, 605c, 606d, 607a
34. *Mein Leben (My Life),* Richard Wagner, pages 415-416.
35. *Plato*, A.E. Taylor, page 211.
36. CD I, page 207.
37. *A History of God,* Karen Armstrong (from *Symposium* translation by W. Hamilton), page 36.
38. *Plato*, A.E. Taylor, page 211.
39. *Wagner on Music and Drama,* Albert Goldman and Evert Sprinchorn, pages 26-27.
40. TC, page 190.
41. *The Ideas of Richard Wagner,* 1988 edition, Allen David Aberback, page 63.
42. TC, page 272.

43. *Elements of the Grail Tradition,* John Matthews, page 205.
44. *Wagner,* Michael Tanner, page 91.
45. *Stories of the Great Operas,* Ernest Newman, page 69.
46. *Kandinski Compositions,* Magdalena Dabrowski,
    N.Y. Museum of Modern Art, 1996.
47. *Mein Leben* (My Life), Richard Wagner, page 522.
48. *The Jesus Mysteries,* Timothy Freke and Peter Gandy, page 80.
49. CL, page 823.
50. TC, page 281.
51. RW VIII, page 312.
52. Ibid, page 305.
53. Ibid, page 318.
54. *Mein Leben (My Life),* Richard Wagner, page 521.
55. *Principles of the Philosophy of the Future,*
    Ludwig Feurnbach, page 53.
56. *Richard Wagner and the Philosophy of the Synthesis of the Arts,*
    Jack Stein, page 68.
57. RW II, page 198, *Opera and Drama.*
58. *Principles of the Philosophy of the Future,* Ludwig Feurnbach,
    pages 54-55.
59. TC, page 50.
60. Ibid, page 50.
61. RW I, page 37.
62. *Richard Wagner's Letters to August Röeckel,* pages 59-60.
63. *Letters to Uhlig, Fisher, and Heine,* Richard Wagner, page 8.
64. *The Life of Richard Wagner,* Ernest Newman II, page 431.
65. *Essays of Thomas Mann,* page 226.
66. *Richard Wagner's Letters to August Röeckel,* page 147.
67. Ibid, page 149.
68. *Götterdamerung das Endes,* Ernest Porter,
    San Francisco Opera *Ring* program.
69. *Richard Wagner's Letters to August Röeckel,* page 108.

70. Ibid, pages 146-147.
71. *Conversations of Goethe with Eckermann,*
    John Peter Eckermann, pages 205-206.
72. *Wagner – Liszt Correspondences (Vol. II),* page 168.
73. *Mein Leben (My Life),* Richard Wagner, page 615.
74. *The World as Will and Idea,* Arthur Schopenhauer,
    pages 110 and 113.
75. Ibid, pages 164 and 169.
76. Ibid, page 168.
77. *The Philosophy of Schopenhauer,* Bryan Magee, page 133.
78. *The World as Will and Idea,* Arthur Schopenhauer,
    pages 167 and 172.
79. *The Philosophy of Schopenhauer,* Bryan Magee, page 372.
80. *The First Hundred Years of Wagner's Tristan,* Elliot Zuckerman,
    pages 32 and 34.
81. *Tristan and the Mystic Expression,* Jeffrey Swann,
    Wagner Society of New York
82. *Then I Myself am the World: Wagner's Opera Metaphysicism,*
    Michael Tanner, Glyndebourne Festival program, 2009,
    page 116.
83. *The Philosophy of Schopenhauer,* Bryan Magee, page 380.
84. *Tristan and the Mystic Expression,* Jeffrey Swann,
    Wagner Society of New York.
85. *Wagner,* Michael Tanner, page 152.
86. Ibid, page 155.
87. *The Life of Richard Wagner,* Ernest Newman (Vol. I), page 418.
88. *The First Hundred Years of Wagner's Tristan,*
    Elliot Zuckerman, page 33.
89. Ibid, page 33.
90. Ibid, page 58.
91. Ibid, page 60.
92. *The Upanishads,* page 13.

93. *Meister Eckhart from Whom God Hid Nothing,*
Forward, page X11
94. *The Upanishads,* page 51.
95. *Meister Eckhart from Whom God Hid Nothing,*
Forward, page 16-17.
96. Ibid, page 68.
97. CD, pages 724-725.
98. Ibid, page 609.
99. RW IV, 29 and 30.
100. CL, page 580.
101. Ibid, page 347.
102. MP, page 118.
103. *The World as Will and Idea,* Arthur Schopenhauer,
page 129.
104. *Parsifal, Lohengrin and the Legend of the Holy Grail,*
Alice Leighton Cleather and Basil Crump, pages 177-178.
105. *The Redeemer Reborn,* Paul Schofield, page 15.
106. *Wagner Rehearsing the 'Ring': An Eyewitness Account
of the Stage Rehearsals of the First Beyreuth Festival,*
Heinrich Porges, page 103.
107. CL, page 425.
108. *Richard Wagner's Letters to August Röeckel,* page 153.
109. CL, page 689.
110. *Parsifal, Lohengrin and the Legend of the Holy Grail,*
Alice Leighton Cleather and Basil Crump, page 110.
111. CL, page 500.
112. *Richard Wagner:* Parsifal, Lucy Beckett, page 13.
113. *Parsifal, Lohengrin and the Legend of the Holy Grail,*
Alice Leighton Cleather and Basil Crump, pages 182-183.
114. *The Household of the Grail,* John Matthews, page 205.
115. *Parsifal: Commentary on CD,* Saul Lilienstein,
Washington National Opera.

116. RW II, pages 349-350.
117. WM, page 33.
118. Ibid, page 129.
119. Ibid, pages 132-133.
120. Ibid, page 143.
121. Ibid, page 150.
122. Ibid, page 158.
123. Ibid, page 143.
124. *Schopenhauer*, Kenneth Hutton, Wagner Society of the United Kingdom, August 2006,   page 10.
125. RAS, page 236.
126. RW I, page 6.
127. *Mein Leben (My Life)*, Richard Wagner, pages 34-35.
128. Ibid, page 42-43.
129. Ibid, page 603.
130. Ibid, page 198.
131. RAS, page 238.
132. Ibid, page 241.
133. RW I, pages 74-75.
134. RAS, page 247.
135. RAS, pages 249-250.
136. *Unbroken Line*, Will Crutchfield.
137. *The Music of the Future*, Richard Wagner, page 33.
138. MP, page 82.
139. *Pro and Contra Wagner*, Thomas Mann, page 219.
140. *Wagner and I Knew Him*, Ferdinand Praeger, page 294.
141. *Essays of Thomas Mann*, page 237.
142. Ibid, page 237.
143. TC, page 258
144. *Wagner and the Wonder of Art: An Introduction to Die Meistersinger*, page 85.

145. *Wagner Writes from Paris,* page 105.
146. Ibid, page 101.
147. *The Ideas of Richard Wagner,* 1988 edition,
     Allen David Aberback, page 347.
148. RW I, pages 68-69.
149. Ibid, page 78.
150. Ibid, page 79.

Have you had a Wagner moment?

If so, please tell us about it.

Wagner Society of Washington, D.C,
P.O. Box 58213
Washington, DC 20037

Fax:
703-370-1924

Email:
webmeister@wagner-dc.org